PHYSICAL EDUCATION IN SCHOOLS

Physical Education in Schools

SECOND EDITION

Edited by
Len Almond

KOGAN PAGE

London • Stirling (USA)

This second edition published in 1997
First published in 1989 as *The Place of Physical Education in Schools*

Kogan Page Limited
120 Pentonville Road
London N1 9JN
and
22883 Quicksilver Drive
Stirling, VA 20166, USA

British Library Cataloguing in Publication Data
A CIP record for this book is available from the British Library.

ISBN 0 7494 1673 4

Typeset by Kate Williams, London.
Printed and bound in Great Britain by Clays Ltd, St Ives plc.

Contents

Notes on the contributors

Len Almond is Senior Lecturer in the Department of Physical Education, Sports Science and Recreation Management at Loughborough University.

David Bunker is Senior Lecturer in the Department of Physical Education, Sports Science and Recreation Management at Loughborough University.

Dr Lorraine Cale is Lecturer in the Department of Physical Education, Sports Science and Recreation Management at Loughborough University.

Bernard Dickenson is Deputy Head, Thomas Telford School.

Jo Harris is Lecturer in the Department of Physical Education, Sports Science and Recreation Management at Loughborough University.

Sonia McGeorge is Deputy Director of the Exercise and Health Research and Development Group at Loughborough University.

Rod Thorpe is Senior Lecturer in the Department of Physical Education, Sports Science and Recreation Management at Loughborough University.

Abbreviations

ASCD	Association for Supervision and Curriculum Development
BAALPE	British Association of Advisers and Lecturers in Physical Education
BHF	British Heart Foundation
CHD	coronary heart disease
DES	Department of Education and Science
DFE	Department for Education
DNH	Department of National Heritage
DoH	Department of Health
HEA	Health Education Authority
HMI	Her Majesty's Inspectorate
HRE	health-related exercise
HRF	health-related fitness
INSET	in-service education of teachers
KS	Key Stage
LEA	Local Education Authority
NC	National Curriculum
NCC	National Curriculum Council
NCPE	National Curriculum for physical education
OFSTED	Office for Standards in Education
RCP	Royal College of Physicians
SCAA	School Curriculum and Assessment Authority
WO	Welsh Office

Preface

In the first edition of this book, *The Place of Physical Education in Schools,* I attempted to develop a basic rationale for physical education and exemplify it through the elaboration of different curriculum areas of physical education. Since its publication a great deal has happened. We have seen the introduction of a National Curriculum, a major national debate with considerable media coverage on sport in schools (together with interventions from John Major) and the introduction of inspections of schools. Yet the messages of 1989 still remain and most of the proposals in that first book are highly relevant today; so why a new edition?

The introduction of a National Curriculum for physical education in many respects constrains the development of a coherent schools programme because it does not outline aspirations which can guide practice and the six activity areas. Thus, this edition expands on a rationale for physical education by creating what could be called *a new vision* of possibilities. The first two chapters outline a new perspective on the role of purposeful physical activities in schools. This is followed by the development of an argument about the context of physical education and how it can promote significant social, moral and emotional dispositions. In the light of current debates about the decline in standards and the need for schools to highlight moral and social concerns, this is an important contribution and a recognition that physical education has a significant part to play. Also, in this third chapter, the point is raised that we need to establish a community to support learning; a community in which there is a shared understanding and commitment to generate a more productive and caring department.

In *The Place of Physical Education in Schools* the idea of *sport education* was highlighted and since then a number of countries, particularly

Australia and New Zealand, have developed major innovations on this theme. Thus I have devoted considerably more space to articulating what is involved in sport education in the hope that teachers will recognize its significance and attempt to develop these ideas in practice. This chapter is followed by three chapters on games, athletics and gymnastics because they represent different dimensions of sport education. The chapters on games by Rod Thorpe and David Bunker and athletics by myself have been retained from the previous edition because their content has still to penetrate the mainstream thinking of teachers. Even though the National Curriculum (in its original state) took on board the thinking behind these two innovations, the theoretical structure and practical implications are still new to some teachers. The ideas in the teaching games for understanding approach represent fundamental issues that penetrate our understanding of sport and therefore need to be revisited. There is much to learn in this important chapter. In the same way, the chapter on athletics is located in the same tradition, but while athletics in schools has hardly changed in the past ten years, club athletics has gone through a major revision and new approaches are emerging. The ideas from the athletics chapter provide a springboard for generating a new direction for school athletics.

The chapter on gymnastics is new, and Lorraine Cale has generated a different perspective and provided some practical guidelines for teachers. In the same way, Jo Harris highlights the importance of a concern for health-related exercise in the curriculum and presents a perspective which can really guide practice.

Sonia McGeorge's outline of the active school is a focal point to generate new initiatives. Teachers need to acknowledge that it is an important part of school life and without such a commitment there is little chance that we will increase the activity patterns of young people . However, I believe that schools can respond to the challenge she proposes and will want to demonstrate that schools really do make a difference.

Finally, Bernard Dickenson explores the idea that Key Stage 4 needs a new focus. It is a crucial part of young people's time in schools and it offers a whole range of new possibilities that can enliven the curriculum, make it more relevant and enhance the status of physical education teachers.

Physical Education in Schools is a starting point for thinking teachers to generate a new perspective on their subject and act as a stimulus to create a better physical education experience for all young people.

Len Almond, 1997

Introduction

The National Curriculum for physical education has been revised and a slimmer version presented to the profession. We have been promised no more changes for the next five years. Does this mean time for consolidation and relief from the numerous changes of recent years, or does it give us the opportunity to reflect critically on the aspirations that guide our actions in schools and attempt to match them with the reality of current practice? I believe it is time to do the latter because the practical concerns of the past few years have dominated our thoughts and left us bereft of a clear direction in which to pursue the richness and potential of physical education for every child.

However, I must take issue with the recommended activity areas articulated in the Orders for the new National Curriculum. The six activity areas appear to represent a balanced physical education programme. What end do these activity areas serve? It is difficult to clearly identify what purposes they serve other than ends in themselves. Thus, to experience athletic activities is simply good because it is identified in the National Curriculum. Why athletics or dance (or any other of the four activity areas) represent significant features of a physical education programme is not elaborated, so it is little wonder that teachers are not tempted to appreciate the roles that they can play in an educational context. They merely have to teach the activity areas because they represent exemplars of what physical education is. Unless teachers are able to elaborate the educational potential of athletics as opposed to swimming, games, dance, outdoor and adventurous activities or gymnastics, and vice versa, they become deliverers of content only.

It is interesting to note that some form of purposeful physical activities are excluded, eg yoga, cycling, all examples of Eastern movement forms such as tai chi, together with sports like judo or wrestling. Circuit training, exercise to music, skipping (jump rope to some), archery or horse riding have no place in the six activity areas. The text of the National Curriculum promotes the idea that health-related exercise should be taught through the activity areas. Thus, the activity areas begin to define physical education as providing a culture to be acquired but not one that can be transformed. Therefore, the National Curriculum for physical education is in danger of paralysing debate about the aspirations that guide practice or at worst stimulating the impression given that there is no need to articulate such aspirations.

Nevertheless, the changing status and position of school sport, dance or adventure-based learning has led to the questioning of their roles in the school curriculum. The requirement for heads of physical education departments to engage in school policy-making has contributed to the feeling that there is a lack of a clear direction for physical education.

In this context there is an urgent need to provide teachers with a framework for a curriculum that incorporates traditional interests and is disciplined by aspirations that can be justified on educational grounds. Thus, this need for an educational rationale for physical education is clearly linked to a curriculum framework that will guide practice. This is not to say that physical education teachers are merely followers and are unable to produce their own rationale. The reality of the current teaching situation and the varying demands on both teachers' time and energy effectively create an environment in which the construction of a coherent statement outlining the value of physical education for young people and its translation into practical exemplars is a complex and demanding task that may seem to be an almost impossible one for many teachers. What is needed is a statement that provides common ground for teachers to debate and to reflect so that their own thinking can be informed by the constructive reactions of their colleagues.

But what are the activities of physical education – the *content* of what we teach? In one sense this is straightforward: physical education consists of a family of activities grouped within four areas – sport, dance, outdoor and adventure-based learning and individual forms of exercise – which are not adequately covered by the previous three areas. These are represented in Figure I.1. They are areas of experience with their own distinctive form, which illustrates something of the richness and the potential of physical education. Sport is concerned with competitive activities whereas dance is concerned with expressiveness in which artistic and aesthetic criteria are employed. These two areas offer qualitatively different experiences and therefore they represent opportunities to explore different dimensions of being physically active. In the same way outdoor and adventure-based learning opens up new avenues of experience for finding satisfaction in physical activity.

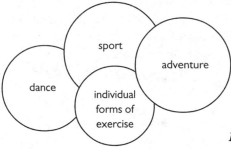

Figure I.1   Four areas of physical education

Teachers are bombarded with a whole host of other demands as areas of physical education identify their claims for a rightful place in the school curriculum. The dance world has elaborated the uniqueness of dance and its educational value in schools. In the 1990 Department of Education and Science (DES) *Interim Report of the Physical Education Working Group for the National Curriculum* (p.13) dance is seen as a distinct art form, with its own history, body of knowledge, aesthetic values, cultural contexts and artistic products. The report goes on to propose that the 'dance as art model' develops in pupils an appreciation of dance as an artistic and aesthetic activity.

This point is reinforced again in 1991 when the Secretary of State for Education proposals for the new National Curriculum for physical education were published. In this document it states that dance:

is an art form and as such is an essential part of a balanced physical education programme. As well as the development of the artistic and aesthetic elements, dance is also concerned with acquiring control, co-ordination and versality in the use of the body, and helps flexibility and develop strength.

It is interesting to highlight two points in this document:

1. The reference to 'our terms of reference made clear that dance was a part of physical education' could suggest that the working group had been informed that dance had to be part of physical education. It is not clear whether this was acceptable to the working group because they could easily have expressed their commitment to such an idea by stating that dance is one part of physical education without any mention of their terms of reference. In the other activity areas such a term is not used.
2. The working group reinforce this point when they propose that dance is an essential part of a balanced physical education pro-gramme. This reference to a 'balanced programme' is not made in any other activity area. It would appear to be some kind of special pleading.

In these influential documents dance is seen as an art form but there appears to be a tension in the location of dance within physical education. This point is reinforced when one reads books on dance. Some argue that it is an art form and make the point that its link with physical education is tenuous. It would seem therefore that the association with physical education is a matter of convenience and managerial necessity.

By placing dance within a physical education programme its potential is likely to be diminished and the time available may well be reduced. Also, a physical education teacher whose main interest lies in sport is less likely to have experience, expertise and commitment to dance, which will reduce its impact. Without such a commitment young people may not have the opportunity to learn to value the activity.

Dance deserves to be an essential element of a young person's curriculum experience in schools and it represents an entitlement of significance – a role that I would not challenge. Whether this role should be part of physical education or an arts curriculum is a controversial debate, but in terms of delivery of the National Curriculum schools have the opportunity to locate dance in any form they deem appropriate. The important point is that all young people should have an entitlement to experience dance during their schooling. However, I believe that it needs to be located more closely within an arts curriculum and kept apart from physical education.

In the same way, I have some concern over outdoor and adventurous activities. Once again the 1990 DES *Interim* report (p.65) provides some guidance as to its role in a school curriculum. It appears to be seen as the opportunity 'to learn skills that will enable them to travel in increasingly demanding environments' and 'to demonstrate leadership and to show awareness of safety in increasingly challenging environments'. Also, it is seen as being associated with risk-taking situations. Later, it is acknowledged that residential experience is an important element of outdoor education but the minimum entitlement may be met through other subjects. This point is reinforced later in the Secretary of State for Education's 1991 proposals for the new National Curriculum for physical education, when it is proposed that outdoor education is a cross-curricular theme and consequently a whole-school responsibility.

I believe that the role of outdoor education and adventurous activities in a school curriculum should be a whole-school issue and not merely hived off to the physical education department. Of course there is much educational value in this area and I am convinced that all young people can benefit significantly from engagement in outdoor/residential living and undertaking adventurous activities in a caring environment. However, as in dance, I believe that its association with physical education needs to be carefully reconsidered. Some aspects of outdoor and adventurous activities can be accommodated within physical education and I shall elaborate these possibilities later, while others such as residential experiences are the concern also of other subjects that may well have a stronger claim.

It is necessary to point out that these distinctive areas – sport, dance and outdoor/adventurous activities – of physical education have something in common. I believe they represent disciplined forms of activity in the sense that there is a great deal to learn in each area, which requires practice and refinement. In order to accomplish anything, commitment, dedication and real effort are involved; at the same time, pursuing these activities generates satisfactions that motivate further participation.

Within physical education these concerns need to be seen as an important priority because attempts to develop ideas about the content of physical education and how they can be implemented need to be seen as the major points of debate. However, teachers need also to be aware of the practical difficulty of developing sport education in addition to the needs of dance education and outdoor and adventure-based learning activities and their combined role in a balanced physical education programme. Perhaps they cannot be completely reconciled and some schools may well see the process of delivery as being a whole-school concern where dance, and perhaps outdoor and adventure-based learning, are undertaken by specialists in a context different to physical education. This debate is a complex one and not easy. My own view is that dance (and also outdoor/adventure-based learning) is too important to be left to the whims of sport-oriented physical education teachers and should have an important role in any school curriculum.

Thus, in the context of this book I am articulating a more narrow view of physical education; nevertheless I believe that this perspective contains a great deal of new thinking and real challenges to the profession that need to be debated thoroughly if we are to generate a new vision for physical education, one that will guide practice and enhance what we offer all young people in school.

REFERENCES

DES (1990) *Interim Report of the Physical Education Working Group for the National Curriculum*, London: DES.

Stevens, S (1992) 'Dance in the National Curriculum' in *New Directions in Physical Education*, vol. 2, N Armstrong (ed.), 141–54. Leeds: Human Kinetics.

CHAPTER ONE

Generating a new vision for physical education

Len Almond

INTRODUCTION

The changing status and position of school sport, dance and adventure-based learning and the subsequent questioning of their roles in the school curriculum, the association with extra-curricular provision and the requirement of heads of physical education departments to engage in school policy-making have contributed to the feeling that there is a lack of a clear direction for physical education. Teachers have been conscious also of the absence of a support structure to enable them to adequately justify physical education and produce a coherent rationale that would stand up to the vigorous questioning of teachers in other departments. The skills of defending one's arguments, writing policy statements and matching aspirations with day-to-day practices go far beyond the traditional strengths of physical education teachers who are used to the practical world of sport and dance.

I shall attempt to sketch out such a direction – a vision of physical education – which will attempt to represent a coherent set of ideals and aspirations that can inform this vision and that I believe the profession could pursue. This vision needs to be translated into a set of strategies that illustrate a process of delivery on how to achieve these aspirations. However, such a strategy must be able to generate a set of practices that never lose sight of the long-term aspirations enshrined in the vision and that exemplify real guides to action and practice. This is a very tall order, so my sketch represents a framework for discussion to enable us to clarify the variety of interpretations that I hope this chapter can generate and that will lead to real guides to practice.

A NEW PERSPECTIVE FOR PHYSICAL EDUCATION

McNamee (1992) and Meakin (1990) clearly located the development of personhood as a principal strand for the aspirations of physical education. In other words physical education in schools in their view should be centrally concerned with the development of personhood and teachers need to reflect critically on how their teaching and learning strategies can contribute towards its promotion. Arnold (1979) McNamee (1995) also argue cogently that the practices of physical education represent *cultural practices of significance* and they present a clearly articulated case for the role of sport in cultural development.

It is these publications that have influenced me considerably in my own deliberations about the values of physical education in our society. They have informed my own articulation of what directions the physical education programme should be aimed at and what focus should be the central stimulus for planning and action. From this perspective I am proposing a framework to guide practice.

First of all my framework for a vision of physical education consists of three central ideas that represent a useful heuristic to focus our attention on the kinds of ideas and aspirations that can guide our actions. The three elements of the framework are:

- Active living.
- Cultural wealth.
- Physicality.

They represent three central aspects of physical education that are interrelated and symbiotic, as well as representing a synergy. What do they involve?

ACTIVE LIVING

'Active living' is a term much used in health promotion but for me it represents an idea that is important to physical education.

Our physical education programmes in schools should be concerned with promoting physical activities because they represent purposeful pursuits that can enrich lives and improve the quality of living. The teacher's task therefore is to help young people acquire a commitment to being active informed by the satisfactions aroused in the pursuit of purposeful physical activity of the kind provided by schools. As a result of finding satisfaction, success and enjoyment in being active within the physical education programme, further participation outside school is stimulated and consequently young people begin to take the first steps in acquiring a commitment to being active. But what are the key components of such a commitment?

Stimulating active living involves:

(a) finding joy in being active
(b) learning to love being active
(c) seeking out active opportunities to enhance one's quality of life
(d) reinforcing one's commitment to being active.

The purposeful activities of physical education provide the means by which we can initiate young people into the richness and potential of active living, which can transform lives and enable them to flourish as persons.

Finally, purposeful physical activity can promote the corporate life of a school by stimulating morale and providing opportunities for teachers, pupils and ancillary staff to find mutual satisfaction in individual and team successes. When schools place a high value on purposeful physical activity it can promote further participation beyond the school.

I would suggest that a central tenet of physical education is that we are striving to encourage young people to see that a commitment to active living is a 'good buy'.

CULTURAL WEALTH

My second element, 'cultural wealth' is directly linked to the first. Sport, dance and adventure pursuits are human practices of great significance and value that affect people in a very pervasive manner and have become a fundamental and important part of human heritage and cultural life. Such activities take up a great deal of media coverage and at certain times international festivals of sporting excellence arouse a great deal of interest generating also considerable political and social debate. In the same way sport, dance and adventure-based activities have inspired the art world to create works that have contributed to a deeper understanding of these cultural forms. These activities have the power to enrich and transform lives, become an absorbing interest that rewards and fulfils, and also provide avenues for the enhancement of human capacities and qualities and the pursuit of excellence.

It has been argued most convincingly by Lawton (1975) and Skilbeck (1984) that one of the tasks of schools is to provide access to, and engagement in, cultural forms and practices so that young people can become acquainted with important and significant features of cultural life. Schools provide the means by which young people can become initiated into sport, dance and adventure activities, which contain rich traditions and exemplify the very best of human endeavour. Coming to understand this scope and recognizing their significance within our culture and tradition is an important aspect of school life. Hence it is important to acknowledge their significance because any form of educational enterprise concerned with such traditions would be incomplete without their inclusion.

There is a certain risk in describing the curriculum in terms of an initiation into a cultural tradition because there is a tendency to represent tradition as something fixed and unchallengeable. Thus, cultural initiation becomes the transmission of the status quo, a commodity handed down from generation to generation. This is far from satisfactory because it is likely that only cultural forms and practices of dominant interests and groups may be promoted and defined exclusively in narrow terms. There is a need to go beyond the simple transmission of cultural forms and examine their transformative power of understanding derived from studying and engaging in such activities as sport, dance or outdoor and adventurous activities. It is important to recognize that over time some traditional activities lose their appeal as interests change, and technological developments occur, which provide the means for new purposeful physical activities to arise. Within society distinctive changes occur and generate new perspectives, which add new dimensions to traditional pursuits.

10

Schools need to recognize their role in stimulating new interest and widening perspectives on the richness and potential of the vast range of pursuits possible. They need to recognize also that the contribution of purposeful physical activities to the enhancement of an individual's quality of life is important because they have the power for enriching life.

Physical education in schools provides the means by which young people can learn how to participate and become involved in purposeful physical activities; they are able to make choices and select activities that can contribute to the enrichment of their lives and add immensely to the quality of living.

At this point it is necessary to acknowledge that purposeful physical activities represent only one curriculum source for enriching, transforming and enhancing the quality of lives. Pupils need to go beyond engagement in a variety of activities, they need also to learn to appreciate and learn *from* their engagement in school activities. Engagement, appreciation and reflection are important processes which enable them to consider in an informed and intelligent way what they can do with their lives and to make decisions about how they choose to spend their time.

PHYSICALITY

The third element in my framework – 'physicality' – is not an easy term because our language does not allow me to express it more clearly. Physicality does not mean 'taming the body' or 'schooling the body' in the sense that physical activity for some people means conditioning the body, submitting it to a form of regimentation or attempting to perfect the body; nor is it a form of curbing the body. It is more an attitude of mind than any kind of activity area, yet it represents a new range of possibilities.

Sport provides opportunities for competitive experiences against others and there is a richness of possibilities within this discipline. Dance also has a wealth of experiences that are distinctly different from competitive sport. However, these disciplines do not adequately cover a range of experiences which are different from competitive sport or expressive (artistic and aesthetic qualities) movement forms. In essence physicality represents a kind of a challenge curriculum and for many people this may well be a better and more appropriate term.

11

Thus, for the purpose of this book I will use the term 'challenge curriculum'. However, the full articulation of physicality needs to be explored in a different context, because I believe it represents an important feature of physical education which has yet to be articulated clearly.

What is a 'challenge curriculum'? It covers all activity areas together with variety of purposeful physical activities not covered by the existing National Curriculum, eg judo and other combat sports, tai chi, rowing, skipping and conditioning activities. It represents also personal striving educational opportunities as opposed to competition against others. Both are a valuable entitlement for all young people; however, in this context only a challenge curriculum is proposed because the competitive curriculum is already clearly understood.

Many people appear to have a need to seek out and face personal challenges in which they can extend themselves, push back personal limits and overcome odds, barriers or fears. It represents an adventure in exploring personal boundaries and potential, and illustrates how people want to demonstrate their competence, explore physical qualities such as endurance or strength, or engage in complex tests that challenge both their physical and mental powers. Yet it can be much more than simply a personal challenge: it can be about extending one's physical capacities and powers into new dimensions. On the other hand, for some people it is not so much a challenge as a need to do something physical and to enjoy being active.

At one extreme it represents a desire to sail single-handed round the world or walk to the centre of Antarctica. At another level some people feel a need to run, swim or cycle a certain distance, perhaps in a particular time – can I do it? Or perhaps it represents the need to be active in the form of a run, a walk or cycle with others or on one's own – even to be solitary – and simply enjoy the satisfaction of being physically active. In the same way, mastering particular movements and practising them for the sheer experience of the movement represents a further dimension of a challenge curriculum.

The framework below attempts to sketch out three main features of a challenge curriculum for physical education.

(a) Seeking out challenge and/or risk in terms of:
  • mastery (of techniques; complex movement forms and skills; getting something right; accomplishing a difficult task);
  • pushing back boundaries (extending personal or externally imposed limits);

- overcoming odds or barriers;
- exploring physical qualities;

(b) Seeking out opportunities to do something physical:
- being active in some way alone or with others;
- being active and feeling at one with environment or surroundings.

(c) Coming to terms with unfolding emotions in the face of challenge and risk:
- overcoming, conquering or suppressing emotions and learning behaviours for coping with, cooling out or reducing emotional reactions that interfere with one's capacity to do something, eg fear in gymnastics.
- picking oneself up after adversity (failure, difficulties).

This brief sketch does not do justice to this idea but I hope to persuade the reader that this element deserves our critical appraisal and exploration of its possibilities. I am simply identifying an aspect of physical education that can easily be overlooked yet it represents an important dimension – it is this aspect of physical education that excites: it creates a personal challenge to be faced and the thrill and satisfaction of trying to master it. There are a number of possibilities which could enlarge our understanding of this dimension of physical education.

We could unite some features of gymnastics, athletics, adventure-based learning, dance and swimming (and others) into a challenge curriculum, though there is no reason why individual activity areas could not retain their own specific challenges. A challenge curriculum represents an organizing idea (or a focus) to build a new vibrant and exciting aspect of the physical education curriculum around it. The challenge curriculum can operate at a personal level and represent an individual form of curricula; it is also possible for group challenges to be devised which provide different forms of learning. Teachers could design a whole range of physical or skill challenges (and creative challenges such as dance motifs and complex skipping or gymnastic routines) with different starting points (relevant to individual needs) set at different levels (simple to complex) with a variety of potential routes (to be chosen by the pupil) that could be followed, thus accounting for differentiation. Continuity and progression can be clearly identified and reward structures built into the tasks. Pupil booklets could be provided to enable everyone to chart their progress and acknowledge their successes. There are many other ways of thinking how the idea of physicality can be delivered in the curriculum and I am sure that teachers can devise creative ways of developing this concept.

What kind of challenges are relevant for such a curriculum? The following categories of challenges could be used as a framework:

(a) Health-related exercise challenges: running, walking, swimming, cycling, skipping, rowing.
(b) Fitness: conditioning challenges.
(c) Sport challenges:
  • individual sports: athletics. swimming, judo, weight lifting, some games
  • team games.
(d) Creative challenges:
  • dance
  • gymnastics
  • synchronized swimming
  • skipping
  • games making.
(e) Adventurous challenges.

The types of challenges are:

1. Participation challenges.
2. Can-do challenges.
3. Improvement challenges.

In addition to fulfilling the general requirements of the National Curriculum, the challenge curriculum incorporates the key components of planning, performing and evaluating.

My three central features of physical education can be made available at any time during school or within any community. There must be good reasons why they are included in the education of young people in schools. These central features of physical education need to be made accessible to the unformed and uninformed minds of young people whose life plans are in the process of unfolding and whose ability to evaluate is not yet well developed. It is for this reason that there is a need to consider the 'educational' role of physical education and its place in schools. This represents a feature of physical education that we tend to forget or ignore, yet it is an important dimension that cannot be overlooked.

14

THE EDUCATIONAL ROLE OF PE

Physical education in schools contributes to the overall education of young people by helping them to learn how to lead full and valuable lives by engaging in purposeful physical activities such as sport, dance, or adventure. These activities can lead to an improvement in the quality of people's lives. They learn to value these activities in a rich and fundamental way by coming to care about them. Schools provide the opportunity for young people to illuminate their understanding of what to do with their lives by helping them to make informed choices about how they could spend their lives and to make sense of their own specific situation. In this case, young people need to learn the following.

1. HOW TO LEAD FULL AND VALUABLE LIVES: SEEKING THE GOOD LIFE AND EXPLORING WHAT IT ENTAILS

Here, the task for teachers is three-fold; we need to:

1. initiate young people into a range of sporting activities which illustrate their significance as important aspects of cultural life – initiating young people into the very best of culturally relevant physical activities;
2. demonstrate how engagement in sporting activities can enrich people's lives and improve its quality; and
3. provide opportunities for students to engage in making decisions about their involvement and commitment to culturally relevant physical activities.

We need to teach sport as one exemplar of a culturally relevant physical activity and demonstrate ways in which sport can contribute to leading a full and valuable life. This would mean that our task is to help young people get on the inside of an activity so that they can learn to value and care about their participation in purposeful physical activity. It would involve learning to acquire positive feelings towards one's participation; in this way a pupil's commitment would create further opportunities for success and satisfaction. It opens up new perspectives on and adds quality (and meaning) to one's life. This represents an important educational role; however, initiation into culturally relevant and purposeful physical activities like sport, dance or adventure-based

15

learning is not enough. We need to find ways of helping young people to learn to make decisions about the role of sport (or dance or adventure-based learning) in their own lives so that they are able to illuminate their understanding of what to do with their lives and how to spend their time.

2. HOW TO ACQUIRE THE POWER TO MAKE DECISIONS

If young people are to make informed decisions about culturally relevant physical activities in their lives, potential barriers need to be recognized and faced so that ways of overcoming them can be explored. Young people need to acquire the power to make decisions rather than have barriers or constraints imposed on them. I once spoke with a girl of 14, Stella (who used to be a keen basketball player) who had little power over what she did. After school she picked up her brother and sister and took them home. She made their tea, occupied the children and did whatever housework or shopping that needed doing until her mother arrived home later in the evening. On Saturday Stella child-minded her brother and sister again while her mother was at work; Sunday was her only free day. In this situation Stella had few opportunities to build organized sport into her life but it was possible to identify ways in which she could be physically active – a self-organized aerobics class at home for her and two other friends twice a week. I know of similar instances where it is a boy who has to be a carer, but it is often older girls who are made to adopt this role. We need to recognize that many young people may experience real barriers that constrain opportunities and inhibit any form of commitment. These need to be examined and alternative strategies need to be explored. There are many types of barriers which may inhibit one's power such as:

- home and parental demands
- little skill in gaining access to opportunities
- peer pressures
- personal pressure such as the feeling that 'I'm not good enough'.

Of course there are many other types but this list serves to illustrate what needs to be done. Acquiring the power to make choices of a certain kind (informed and rational) and arrived at in a certain way (ie, non-coercive and non-indoctrinatory) requires allowing time in the curriculum for young people to explore and recognize the constraints on their capacity to fit purposeful physical activity into their lives. It is not enough just to provide young people with opportunities to acquire competence and confidence in a range of sports. We need to recognize that our professional skill goes beyond this: we have to take account of our role in stimulating further participation in sport, dance or adventure-based activities beyond the school. From an 'educational' perspective many young people may need additional help in translating meaningful school-based opportunities into reality outside of school.

PEDAGOGY: THE MISSING INGREDIENT

In summary, physical education entails the promotion of active living (stimulating and sustaining a commitment to being physically active) which generates well-being (enrichment and flourishing through what Strike (1990) calls the 'goods of accomplishment'). This can be represented in the following way:

Values	Content
Personhood (flourishing)	Sports curriculum
Cultural wealth (enrichment)	Challenge curriculum

In terms of health-related exercise, promoting an active living perspective provides a climate for stimulating further participation in purposeful physical activities beyond the curriculum. However, this climate also represents a process in which a teacher's pedagogy is critical. Underpinning these values is a commitment to the 'every child' concept. In this concept I am suggesting that teachers need to recognize that every child:

- is important
- can be good at purposeful physical activity
- can learn
- can achieve success and make progress
- can achieve satisfaction
- can acquire confidence
- can recognize their own self-worth
- is entitled to sample the best of physical education.

17

For such a pedagogy to be effective teachers must believe in a commitment to the every child concept and their practice needs to match this commitment. Teachers need to provide opportunities for:

(a) Physical activity to be: fun, exciting and purposeful (it has a point, it leads somewhere) and not a form of aversion therapy.

(b) A real challenge with mastery possibilities : this involves learning to answer a task (which has a point or focus) with clear targets which:
  • are visible, manageable and attainable,
  • lead to achievement, progress and confidence,
  • generate self-worth. It is important to point out that such challenges need to be based first on personal striving (can do, participation or creative challenges) and if pupils wish to extend their competence and compete against others it should be something that they wish to opt into and not something they are made to do.

(c) Activity that is personalized and accommodates differentiation principles such as:
  • matching tasks with different capabilities, abilities, needs and interests
  • making provision for different
    – starting points
    – rates of progress
    – routes
    – outcomes
    – motivations within a class
  • recognizing the need for management/organization styles that accommodate variety and diversity.

(d) Pupils to obtain positive feedback from teachers and peers.

(e) Pupils to work productively within a clear structure that is consistent and provides support, constant encouragement and justified praise.

(f) Teachers to ensure that they make regular contact with *all* children. How can pupils make progress without direct contact at some stages in the learning process? Yet this simple point is difficult to achieve in practice.

(g) Pupils to:
  • learn from doing (planning, performing and evaluating),
  • share in the learning process through helping others and learn-

ing with and from others (this may involve peer education or child-to-child approaches),

- learn to acquire independence, and
- experience a sense of ownership of their work.

It is important to recognize that such a pedagogy needs a school rewards structure with motivation schemes (personal and social) and a recognition system (by the whole school, individual teachers and peers).

How can we develop school structures and professionally competent teachers who can deliver this? This question brings us back full circle. If the physical education profession is to pursue the richness and potential of physical education for every child it needs to ensure that there are opportunities first, to reflect critically on the aspirations that guide our actions in schools and second, such deliberations need to consider the reality of current practice and the constraints it places on the development of an authentic physical education. In this chapter I have attempted to provide a framework in which teachers can reflect critically and take the first steps in translating complex aspirations into real practice within schools.

CONCLUSION

In this chapter I have sketched out a new framework for re-examining physical education. For many people it may represent a narrower focus than they would like; however, this narrowness only refers to the titles under which we organize a whole range of experiences. By eliminating the need for specific activity areas, I hope that teachers can be freed from its constraints and start looking at the nature of the experiences that physical education can offer.

In addition, I have attempted to highlight the educational role of physical education and to present also the need for a pedagogy of practice which I refer to as the missing ingredient in physical education. Pedagogy is a truly missing ingredient and I would argue very strongly that a commitment to its principles will enhance physical education and make it a better experience for all young people.

REFERENCES

Arnold, P (1979) *Meaning in Movement, Sport and Physical Education*, Oxford: Heinemann.

Lawton, D (1975) *Class, Culture and the Curriculum*, London: Routledge & Kegan Paul.

McNamee, M (1992) 'Physical education and the development of personhood', *Physical Education Review* **15**(1), pp.13–28.

McNamee, M (1995) 'Sporting practices, institutions and virtues: a critique and a restatement', *Journal of Philosophy of Sport*, **XXII,** pp.61–83.

Meakin, D C (1990) 'How physical education can contribute to personal and social education', *Physical Education Review* **13**(2), pp.108–19.

Skilbeck, M (1984) *School-based Curriculum Development*, London: Harper & Row.

Strike, K (1990) 'The legal and moral responsibility of teachers' in *The Moral Dimensions of Teaching*, J I Goodlad *et al.* (eds), San Francisco, CA: Jossey-Bass.

CHAPTER TWO

The context of physical education

Len Almond

Strike (1990) makes an important point when he writes, 'These activities (in terms of physical education, purposeful physical activities) are not only the means for realising the "goods of accomplishment", they are also the context for friendships and community'. Even though Strike is not speaking about physical education his point is very important. Thus, for me, physical education should not be merely concerned with its *content* – the 'goods of accomplishment' – there is another important aspect that is often neglected, forgotten or even ignored: ie is the *context* in which there are opportunities for interpersonal competences to be acquired, appreciated and shaped as a result of interactions with others, and in this process enable one to achieve an understanding of their relevance.

In this chapter I propose to elaborate how the context of teaching physical education can be used to promote important educational values. These values are associated with social, moral and emotional dispositions. First of all I shall discuss their importance and relevance and this will be followed with an outline of a framework to guide practice.

SOCIAL AND MORAL VALUES

> One can realise the end of life, the good life, each and every day
> by living with a liberal spirit, showing equal respect to all citi-
> zens, preserving an open mind, practising tolerance, cultivating
> a sympathetic interest in the needs, interests and struggles of
> others, imagining new possibilities, protecting basic human
> rights and freedoms, solving problems with the method of intel-
> ligence in a non-violent atmosphere pervaded by a spirit of
> co-operation. These are primary among the liberal virtues.
> (Quote from Steven Rockefeller in Taylor, 1992, pp.87–98)

This statement inspired this chapter. In order to fulfil such aspirations it is important to take stock of everything that we do in our teaching to establish that the experiences that we plan support our educational purposes rather than undermine them. In this sense teachers in
schools need to look at themselves through a kind of ethical lens and
consider how everything that goes on in school affects the values and
character of our pupils. To create an environment that nourishes values
and relationships is central to the challenge of creating an ethical community.

In such an ethical community we need to build a consensus on the
values that are important – a basis on which people can move forward
together. We cannot impose anything on people because this would
destroy the real essence of generating an ethical community that cares
about its members. Such a consensus must express people's aspirations
and offer a framework for transforming the current ad hoc arrange-
ment in which ethical and social concerns represent simply a spin-off
from what some would see as 'the real concerns of teaching physical
education' – sporting competence. It needs also to speak a language of
empathy and understanding so that individuals in the department find
themselves and their desires clearly visible within it. In the minds of
the teachers an ethical community's consensus must rest on desire
rather than guilt, addressing issues that can give substance and back-
bone to the consensus. From this consensus teachers need to feel a commitment to implementing it, the will to carry it out and finally the
behaviour that clearly demonstrates they care about it.

I believe that all experiences within physical education should be
aligned so that they support the values that a school cares about rather

than undermine them. We need to generate a process that lets teachers rediscover the values that really matter to them, establish some common ground that enables them to explore how they can be implemented and lead towards procedures that reinforce them. However, in the absence of any whole-school consensus the physical education department can lead the way by demonstrating how the process can be generated and articulated into a common framework for action. This would represent a major achievement for any physical education department and illustrate its potential in promoting ethical and social values.

There is a problem in this argument: it is easy to assume that if only we held the right values our problems would be solved. Endorsing a particular set of values doesn't give one as much guidance as you might think. They need translating into actual practices. Thus we need to ask how can teachers generate a set of values that can inspire and guide their practice.

In the USA a 1992 character education conference (The Aspen Declaration) identified six values: respect, responsibility, trustworthiness, caring, justice and fairness, and civic virtue and citizenship (ASCD, 1995). Others have outlined seven traits: courage, loyalty, justice, respect, hope, honesty and love. Such lists may serve as a starting point for discussion and critical reflection on the values that individual members of a department might hold and wish to use both as an inspiration and a guideline to practice. But there needs to be some caution and recognition that a list of values or virtues does not give you the psychological equipment to abide by any of them. Lists appear safe but they are far too simplistic and when we try to enrich them and elaborate them into real guidelines we may find that conflict and disagreements emerge to unsettle the discussion.

Whatever the dangers of using a list of values as a starting point, it is necessary for teachers to explore what it is that they value and which expresses their ethical aspirations for young people. The fact that we have spent so little time articulating such values and determining what they mean in practice should not deter us from engaging in such an important enterprise. Nevertheless, it is easy to propose that such action is taken and stand aloof without offering any concrete assistance. Carr (1991) and Meakin (1994) can provide much food for thought and stimulate more informed discussion. The profession, through its national organizations and institutes of higher education must accept more responsibility and provide opportunities for serious debate so that all of us (teachers, lecturers, advisers, administrators and students) can collaborate in the process of articulating a clear vision of the potential of physical education.

At present the profession appears merely to endorse a managerial curriculum of activity areas which represent a limited conception of physical education's potential and leaves to discretion the most pressing needs of the day. The publication by SCAA of a National Forum for Values in Education and the Community has raised the possibility that a consensus statement may stimulate teachers to generate guidelines for their schools. This is an important initiative that needs translating into practical steps, once the document has been seriously digested and thoroughly discussed.

There are other points that need to be raised here. An ethical consensus within physical education needs to consider replacing discipline based on rewards and punishment with values that young people can learn to associate with. We must know in our minds, our hearts and our spirit that hurting others is wrong; children must learn that they cannot do what they want as long as they don't get caught or that they should perform a kind deed only if they get a reward. In the same way negative language like 'Don't be late', 'Don't do that' or 'Don't forget' should be translated into explicit positive language. These are simple messages, but they represent important elements in a move towards guidelines that inspire and inform good practice.

We need to be aware also that bad behaviour by young people is not a consequence of their not holding the right values. The notion that behaviour follows values in some unmediated way is incorrect. If you are behaving badly it doesn't mean you have bad values: many people who hold good values can behave badly.

Young people need to receive a consistent message, and feel safe and secure that they have contributed towards the framing of a policy on behaviour based on principles. They need to learn what these values mean and why they are important, and we have to hold pupils (and staff) accountable in some way so that when they violate the value there is some form of sanction and they recognize and acknowledge that they're responsible for their behaviour. A pupil who has neither self-discipline nor empathy will not be able to abide by any values, so for me, learning and acquiring an ethical capacity presumes these two characteristics. Building such influential relationships in a school environment is central to the challenge of ethical education. To teach such values without resorting to preaching and didacticism is a great skill of teaching.

A FRAMEWORK OF GOOD PRACTICE

Moving on from a discussion of social and ethical issues and translating them into a practical framework for action is not easy. This framework represents an attempt to provide a set of features that highlight key aspects of interpersonal competence. Thus, for me the *context* of physical education provides opportunities for three distinct aspects to emerge.

I. THE 'GOODS OF RELATIONSHIP' (WITH PEERS AND TEACHERS)

Relationships in physical education are concerned with three key features: social learning and relationships; learning to care and respect others; and acquiring a sense of belonging.

(a) Social learning and relationships
  - learning to work productively with others
  - establishing reciprocity with others
  - cooperating with others on tasks
  - sharing and planning within the learning process with others
  - learning with and from others.
(b) Caring about others/acquiring respect for others
  - caring, consideration of others, unselfishness
  - trust and respect for others
  - fairness and tolerance
  - sensitivity to others.
  Such dispositions can only emerge within a caring atmosphere in which there is a strong sense of belonging to a community (a sense of shared committed experience).
(c) Developing a sense of belonging.

In developing positive relationships with others one of the main ingredients that reinforces their significance is the *sense of belonging* to a group, whether it is as a member of a team, a class unit or a small community of learners. It is important that teachers recognize the need for young people to feel part of a group so that in building relationships and learning to share and cooperate with others they begin to learn that belonging to a group brings its own rewards. In the same way a sense of belonging reinforces caring about others and treating them with respect.

2. CONDUCT AND RELATIONSHIPS

In the context of sport this is a particularly important concern. The central feature of conduct is the need to promote fairness and tolerance; this entails helping pupils refrain from:

- breaking rules deliberately
- seeking to gain unfair advantages
- exploiting situations for one's own selfish desire
- taking unacceptable actions such as intimidation, direct aggression, verbal abuse or disagreements with officials, and recognizing that taking positive action promotes a better game.

3. EMOTIONS AND FEELINGS IN INTERACTION WITH OTHERS

In developing the idea of promoting positive relationships we need to recognize the role of emotions – the way we react to others and the feelings that emerge from interaction with others in a variety of quite diverse situations. It is possible to construct a kind of positive and negative list of emotions:

Positive		*Negative*	
joy	satisfaction	fear	tension
contentment	modesty	hate	pride
love	wonder	anger	remorse
sympathy	excitement	shame	anxiety
hope	exhilaration	envy	grief
elation	awe-struck	regret	disappointment

These emotions can emerge in the context of establishing relationships with others but teachers need professional skills in promoting positive emotions and helping young people learn to cope with negative emotions. In the same way, teachers and parents who are concerned about emotional behaviours, will want to know how to deal effectively with emotional upheavals, outbursts, reactions, disturbances or maybe those pupils who we believe have clouded or even warped emotions. The pedagogical process of dealing with emotions in social contexts may entail helping pupils to cool off, reducing emotional states, or helping pupils to cope with specific emotions, but it may also be about eliciting emotional responses, refining, channelling, sharpening and maybe heightening emotions. In this way, the professional skill of the teacher as a facilitator or the provider of a rich and stimulating environment suitable for the unfolding of emotions becomes a major pedagogical requirement. This brief sketch serves to illustrate something of the complex nature of emotions and their educational potential – a potential that physical education teachers can fulfil.

In this context I would like to propose that the teachers' professional skill lies in being able to adopt strategies which allow them to:

Reach out to pupils – helping young people with cooling out or to overcome, conquer, cope with, reduce, or suppress potentially negative feelings or destructive emotions; also helping pupils to identify and deal with insufficiency.

Draw pupils out – eliciting and channelling positive and productive qualities.

Stretch pupils – helping pupils to move beyond current standards by challenging them in the process of refining, sharpening and channelling emotional states and finally translating them into educational experiences.

In each one of these aspects of the *context* of physical education there are important interpersonal dispositions to be acquired, shaped and appreciated. There is much learning that needs to be accomplished and physical education can provide significant opportunities for getting to know oneself as a person through personal encounters with the 'goods of accomplishment' as well as 'goods' that can be generated in interaction with others.

AN EDUCATIONAL ROLE IN THE PROMOTION OF INTERPERSONAL COMPETENCE

When one takes on board the ideas presented in this section, the educational task of physical education becomes extensive. Teachers are the shapers of uninformed and unformed minds, therefore decisions about what to do and how to achieve it are grounded in ethical decisions. This makes the process of planning and mapping opportunities for young people to encounter the goods of accomplishment and also the goods of relationships worthy of our best deliberations and the need for informed debate. It is important, however, to recognize that our deliberations need to take into account quite deliberately how the context of physical education is a powerful medium for promoting interpersonal competence. Without such deliberations and concern for interpersonal competences we provide an impoverished curriculum. Thus the educational role in the *context* of physical education is concerned with *removing the distortions to a person's self-respect created by significant others*.

The crucial feature of human life is fundamentally dialogical. We become full human agents capable of understanding ourselves (hence defining our identity) through interaction with what George Herbert Mead called 'significant others'. Our identity is defined in dialogue with, sometimes in struggle against, what others want to see in us.

We are partly shaped by recognition or misrecognition by people we come into contact with on a regular basis. A person or group of people can suffer real damage or distortion from people around them who may mirror back a confining, demeaning or contemptible picture of them. It is believed that people can internalize a picture of their own inferiority or poor self-respect from significant others, so that they may well be incapable of taking advantage of new opportunities. Their own self-depreciation becomes one of the most potent instruments of their own oppression. Thus, an important role that teachers can play is to help young people purge themselves of this imposed and destructive identity.

This is a very important professional role of the teacher in the same way that another of their roles is to help individuals to recognize limitations in performances or in attempts to achieve something (which may lead to a sense of failure) and provide opportunities to re-build and overcome obstacles.

In this process of acquiring, shaping and learning to appreciate interpersonal dispositions, significant others (teachers and pupils) within the school's community become important dimensions. They can be shapers of positive images or they can generate distortions of a person's self or identity. It is crucial that teachers work towards the removal of such distortions in inter-personal learning and encourage all young people to help each other in the process of shaping positive images of a person's self. Helping young people in this way is an important feature of our commitment to help each other, pupils and teachers.

One of the important lessons that I learnt while watching a group of 11-year-old boys and girls playing football was the need for positive social skills. Each time someone did something wrong one person (sometimes a few) would make derogatory comments which reduced the offender's view of their competence and lowered their self-worth. It was clear that these young people did not know how to help each other; here was a marvellous learning opportunity for interpersonal dispositions that could support and nurture the 'goods of accomplishment'.

This is one simple example but it helps to illustrate the potential of positive social relationships. It convinced me that we need to work at producing exemplars for making such situations real educational opportunities.

When one examines how we could develop situations to help young people learn to cope with feelings and emotions it is obvious that there is much potential. It is this kind of work that needs to be done now that the statutory orders are in place and we can expect no new statutory changes for at least five years. Surely this is a challenge worth taking up?

This can only be accomplished in a community in which there is a shared commitment to action with common understanding of the significant task in hand. One commentator on the National Forum for Values in Education and the Community made a similar point in an editorial, stressing the importance of 'collective endeavour for the common good of society' (*The Guardian*, 31 October 1996).

DEVELOPING A COMMUNITY TO SUPPORT LEARNING

Though the *content* (the physical activities that pupils engage in) and *context* (the situations in which pupils encounter and engage in physical activities) of physical education can generate significant opportunities for promoting a person's well-being, this may only be achieved by creating a community (in this case within a school) in which this can unfold.

This process entails a shared commitment in which every individual (teachers and pupils) must be allowed and enabled to contribute to the community. Donald Soper claims that 'you change society to make people better, not the other way round' (*The Guardian*, 21 January 1993). There is a great deal of insight in this statement and it has particular relevance for the idea of a caring community. You can only (or you are more likely to) behave responsibly or learn to care about others if the environment permits it or encourages it.

Strike (1990) believes, and it is a view that I share, that caring is a central good and lies at the root of many others, and he proposes that 'no coherent view of a desirable human life can simply reject it' (p.215). He goes on to say 'Many of the goods of relationships are highly dependent on the goods of accomplishment for their realisation', which reinforces the point made earlier that, in addition to the content of physical education, the context can be a powerful tool for learning valuable and desirable dispositions. However, in schools where teachers deal with many young people at the same time, it is necessary to have also a concern for justice, for the distribution of scarce goods, in the sense that there is competition for the teacher's time.

It is the environment of learning (and caring) that teachers create that is necessary to make available the 'goods of accomplishment and relationships'. In this nurturing and cultivating process teachers are engaged in:

- identifying strategies for promoting learning
- creating a sense of belonging
- presenting models of morally acceptable behaviours
- involving pupils in the construction of rules of conduct
- helping pupils participate in the school community
- helping pupils recognize their role in supporting the learning of others.

However, this cannot be achieved unless the teacher recognizes the need to scaffold the learning process in order to ensure that young people are empowered to acquire interpersonal dispositions. We need to create the conditions that generate collegiality and solidarity in order to move towards such a community, which:

- values all individuals
- promotes fairness for all in the distribution of scarce goods
- encourages trust and respects everyone
- creates a caring and considerate atmosphere
- is tolerant and sensitive towards individual differences, needs and interests
- fosters reflection on the consequences of personal actions and collective responsibility

- stimulates the growth of a constructive sense of the person through one's interactions and relationships with others.

All of these ideas are based on an understanding that within a community teachers need to adopt a caring pedagogy that encompasses a set of procedural principles to guide one's practice and that will protect and promote children's interests and welfare. There needs to be a school and department policy in which pupils and teachers have been involved in framing guidelines. This process of negotiation is central to providing a support for the personal development of every child. It is important that the environment, the climate or the ethos of the physical education community in a school is concerned with:

- teacher expectations of acceptable behaviour
- rules that govern conduct (pupils need to be involved in their creation)
- models of morally acceptable standards of behaviour
- models of caring behaviour
- reward structures that support/reinforce caring and morally acceptable standards of behaviour.

Without these a community can not exist and children's learning will be impoverished. However valuable we may regard these components, the environment of learning and teaching needs to be carefully considered. Just as teachers plan a scheme of work to establish continuity, development and coherence across a Key Stage for each activity area (and the 'goods of accomplishment'), I would argue that teachers also need to plan how they can create a suitable school structure to generate a sense of community (a sense of shared committed experience) to realize the 'goods of relationships'.

Such a community is centred on a belief that it is necessary to generate a set of common purposes and shared understandings about the enterprise of creating a learning environment and adopting appropriate teaching approaches. In this sense the community is attempting to create procedures that lead to successful common action in which it should follow that a pedagogy of care needs to inform our practices. It is essential that we make adequate provision for teachers to acquire a caring pedagogy, an informed and intelligent 'practical knowledge base' and adequate opportunities for them to feel confident and competent in making available the very best of physical education to all young people. Such a proposal needs a radical appraisal of current provision and a search for new ways of reaching schools and teachers and generating a sense of belonging to a profession that stimulates a real love of purposeful physical activity and a desire to reach all young people.

CONCLUSION

Finally, how do I translate such ideas into practical guidelines? Lawrence Stenhouse, in the development of the Humanities Curriculum Project (HCP) and the English version of the American Social Studies project, MAN: A Course of Study, modified Peters' notion of 'principles of procedure' to identify a set of principles to guide practice. This was developed even further by John Elliott in the Ford Teaching Project to evolve a set of procedural principles that could be used to both examine practice and to develop it. It is this notion that provides one possible key to producing guidelines that can be translated into action. It involves working out what teachers need to do in a positive sense to promote something (positive principles) and what teachers need to refrain from doing (negative principles) in their practice. As a result, a set of procedural principles can be drawn up:

PRINCIPLES OF PRACTICE

Positive enabling practices	*Negative inhibiting practices*
+	−
Continue to do:	Refrain from:

In one sense such principles are a form of technocratic guidelines, but I am proposing that they enable us to provide principles that can actually guide practice. Some people will argue that good teachers do this already; they may well do so, but this misses the point: we are trying to enhance everyone's practices, particularly for the 'goods of relationships'.

What I have produced is only the beginnings of an idea. It is untested, its logic and structure need further expansion, but it provides us with a starting point to generate more comprehensive guidelines. We need to articulate essential features or characteristics of each key principle as it relates to specific areas of physical education and attempt to define positive and negative principles to form a basis for a set of guidelines. Where does this takes us? I believe that this route is worth pursuing because it enables us to articulate a set of guidelines that we can build into our teaching.

REFERENCES

ASCD (1995) 'The content of their character', *Curriculum Update*, April 1995.

Carr, D (1991) *Educating the Virtues*, London: Routledge.

Elliott, J (1976–77) 'Developing hypotheses about classrooms from teachers' practical constructs: an account of the Ford Teaching Project', *Interchange* **7**(2). Ontario Institute for Studies in Education.

Meakin, D (1994) 'The emotions, morality and physical education', *Physical Education Review* **17**(2), pp.106–16.

Meed, G H (1984) *Mind, Self and Society*, Chicago: Chicago University Press.

Peters, R S (1966) *Ethics and Education*, London: George Allen & Unwin.

SCAA (1996) 'Education for adult life: the spiritual and moral development of young people', SCAA Discussion Papers, no. 6.

Stenhouse, L (1983) *Authority, Education and Emancipation*, London: Heinemann Educational Books.

Strike, K (1990) 'The legal and moral responsibility of teachers' in *The Moral Dimensions of Teaching*, J I Goodlad *et al.* (eds), San Francisco, CA: Jossey-Bass.

Taylor, C (1992) *Multiculturalism and The Politics of Recognition*, Princeton NJ: Princeton University Press.

CHAPTER THREE

Sport education in schools

Len Almond

INTRODUCTION

Sport can be miseducative as well as an educational experience. Thus, it is important in schools to present sport as an opportunity to help all young people become what Daryl Siedentop (1994) calls 'competent, literate and enthusiastic sports people'. He goes on to propose that sport provides opportunities for all young people to learn to value fair play, to respect both opponents and officials and to appreciate how an evenly contested game enables all of us to experience the beauty of a well-played game – a point that Arnold (1979) captures so vividly in his portrayal of two competitors in a game.

In the 1980s I listened to a lecture given by Daryl Siedentop from Ohio State University in which he outlined his ideas for enhancing the quality of the sport experience in schools. His ideas made strong connections with the games education ideas extolled in the Teaching Games for Understanding movement of that period (see Rod Thorpe, Chapter 4), provided a new avenue for its development and created a wider perspective. Since then Siedentop's ideas have been developed further in New Zealand (Grant *et al.*, 1992) and in Australia (Alexander and Taggart, 1995) and generated much interest as these innovations have been well received and the evaluation reports successful.

The inspiration for sport education arose from Daryl Siedentop's original proposal and the developments of the Teaching Games for Understanding approach at Loughborough University. In this chapter, I set out a framework for promoting sport education.

MAKING THE CASE FOR SPORT EDUCATION

I made the point in Chapters 1 and 2 that sporting activities have the power to enrich and transform lives, become an absorbing interest that rewards and fulfils, and provide avenues for the enhancement of human capacities and qualities, and the pursuit of excellence. Consequently, these sporting activities have become human practices of great significance and value that affect people in a very pervasive manner and have become a fundamental and important part of human heritage and cultural life. The significance of these activities means that a great deal of media coverage is devoted to sport and at certain times international festivals of sporting excellence arouse a great deal of national interest and generate considerable political and social debate.

How should we present sport to young people? I would like to propose that we should focus our attention on the idea of sport education. The task for teachers is three-fold. We need to:

1. initiate young people into a range of sporting activities that illustrate their significance as important aspects of cultural life;
2. demonstrate how engagement in sporting activities can enrich people's lives and improve its quality; and
3. provide opportunities for students to engage in making decisions about their involvement and commitment to sport.

We need to teach sport as one exemplar of culture and how sport can contribute to a young person's education. This portrayal of the value of sport raises an expectation for schools. Simply presenting a range of sports to young people each year and expecting connections between sports to be made is not good enough. We have to go beyond a rather simplistic model in which techniques are often taught in isolation and the presentation of sport is seen as a series of small blocks of different

g activities with little continuity or progression. Thus, in year
boys of 11 are likely to encounter soccer, rugby, cricket, athletics,
cross-country running, gymnastics and perhaps swimming. Girls would
encounter netball, hockey and rounders. In some schools boys and girls
may well be taught together. Following this pattern in years 8–11, the
major changes would be the introduction of a wider range of games as
pupils are given the opportunity to experience different sorts of games
and more individual sports with some element of choice.

What should we do to replace the current model of sport in which we
teach specific activity areas in isolation? Often very little attempt is
made to see them as different examples of sport that illustrate the richness and the potential of a significant cultural practice – in this case
sport. I would like to propose that we reconsider how we teach individual sporting activities and think about producing an organizing
focus for bringing together all our sporting activities within the curriculum. This organizing focus needs to have form and content if it is to
match any idealized expectations for sport.

A CLASSIFICATION SYSTEM FOR SPORT EDUCATION: PRINCIPLES OF SELECTION

In order to change this state of affairs, I would like to propose that
teachers consider the idea of sport education instead of teaching a wide
variety of discrete sporting activities. Sport education enables the
teacher to present an argument for why they have chosen particular
sporting activities. This is important because the selection of sports
needs to be based on guiding principles rather than some arbitrary
choice. We need to identify principles that enable us to sample and select activities that are representations of distinctive types of sport:
there is so much to choose from and individual sports offer very different experiences for young people.

Alderson (1982) and Alderson and Critchley (1990) provide us with a
useful way of making a selection of activities. They suggest the following sport activity types, which are based on distinctive forms of ability
and represent distinct aspects of motor control:

coincidence anticipation	*pattern replication*	*power production*
– games	– gymnastics	– athletics

This classification system outlines a range of sports in the form of categories or families of activities with similar characteristics. As there is an enormous range of sporting possibilities with only limited resources in terms of facilities, staffing, finance and time, it is appropriate to use such a classification as a basis for allocating different kinds of sports to a particular category of sport type and making a selection for inclusion in the curriculum. However, how do we select which sports to use in order to sample the richness and potential of sport?

This richness and potential is exemplified in the three categories outlined above. In games the outcome of the contest is based on the skilfulness and tactical awareness of a team or individual in scoring more points or goals than their opponents. Games are very different from gymnastics in which how you perform the movement – the execution of a gymnastic skill with a particular level of difficulty – is crucial to the appraisal of the activity and its outcomes. This appraisal is based on aesthetic criteria and in this sense they portray gymnastics as a judgmental sport. This category is often referred to as aesthetic sports (Best, 1978). In games, how you perform is not crucial to the result of the contest. In the same way, the outcome of athletics, and the manner of achieving it, is based on maximizing one's performance to exceed that of your opponent or opponents, which is very different from games or gymnastics. Alderson (1982) outlines a number of other criteria such as structure, strategy, technique and demands to illustrate specific differences in sports. In this way, his classification system provides criteria of selecting activities as representatives of distinct categories of sport. It is likely that there are other productive classification schemes that could be used also as principles of selection.

The outline below represents an illustration of how sports can be classified into categories:

Classification of sport types
Main focus – competition against others

Games
co-incidence anticipation

Use of an object

target invasion	net/wall	fielding/run scoring

Fighting games

judo	wrestling	fencing

Aesthetic sports

rhythmic gymnastics	artistic gymnastics	sport acrobatics
trampoline	diving	ice dance
figure skating	ballroom dancing	surfing
dressage	synchronized swimming	

Power production

athletics	swimming	cycling
skiing	orienteering	rowing
canoeing	cyclo-cross	weight lifting
speed climbing		

In the case of games, the idea of principles of selection can be taken further so that a selection of different game forms can be made in order to sample the best of games. This is a central feature of the Teaching Games for Understanding approach. When one considers the other two categories it is not as easy to identify clearly key principles of selection. However, this task needs to be explored and developed further if a coherent principles of selection approach is to be created.

FOUR FEATURES OF SPORT EDUCATION

Once teachers have made their selection of sports, what features should they emphasize in addition to mastery of techniques and skills that are fundamental to sporting achievement? The following features are important aspects of learning about sport and engagement in its traditions and practices. Within sport education I recognize four components.

I. CELEBRATING SPORTING ENDEAVOUR THROUGH FESTIVALS

One of the attractions of sport within cultural traditions is a festival or a bringing together of competitors to share in the satisfactions aroused by participating in that sport, or to provide the opportunity for people to challenge worthy opponents. The culminating nature of a festival provides a base for teachers to use as a representation of major sporting events, but also as a means of bringing together everything that needs to be learnt for sport education.

2. LEARNING ROLES AND RESPONSIBILITIES IN SPORT PARTICIPATION

Sport involves different roles such as performer, official and leader/ coach. Within a festival there are performers, coaches who support them and have been involved in the preparation for the events, and officials who oversee the conduct of the competitions. It is important that young people recognize that sport requires people who will adopt different roles and who will serve different functions in the promotion of sport. Schools can provide the means by which young people have the opportunity to experience different roles in order to recognize their significance, but also to learn the different satisfactions that can be gained from participation as an official or a coach. In addition, it would be appropriate to provide opportunities for learning to be an informed spectator.

In school, young people engage in sport usually as performers and this is right, but there comes a time when it is necessary to provide the opportunity for them to act as a coach or leader of a small group preparing for a tournament, and also to learn how to be an official. When young people are in their final two years of secondary education, some may decide that acting as a sports official is what they would choose to do as a leisure pursuit rather than being a performer. It is therefore important that we consider how we can make provision for such interests (or stimulate such interests). Obviously this will create many difficulties in terms of organizing the acquisition of knowledge and experience for such roles and this must not be underestimated, but if we value the need to teach young people about the richness and potential of sport this is necessary.

In addition, schools need to recognize the value of helping young people to become informed and intelligent spectators and intelligent students of sport (first in the form of being absorbed in the collection of information about a sport, and secondly as a student studying for an examination such as GCSE).

3. LEARNING TO COMPETE AND WHAT CONSTITUTES COMPETITION

- The role of rules in competition (structure, equality, protection, conduct).

39

- What makes a 'good' competition.
- Acquiring morally acceptable attitudes in sporting behaviour.

This is a major aspect of sport education, given that competition is a necessary condition for sport. However, there is much confusion and misunderstanding about its use. I therefore propose to articulate a view of competition that I believe provides much scope for considering what has to be learnt in an education that involves competitive sport.

In any sport, we need to teach young people how to compete and what competition involves. However, there is considerable confusion about the meaning of competition and teachers need to understand some important principles.

Sport involves competition against others. It is concerned with either a physical problem, eg in a game like soccer, or a challenge, eg athletics. Games such as soccer represent a problem-solving activity in which we employ tactics and skill to solve the problems presented by our opponents. A competition has three elements:

1. rules that set out what the game (eg soccer) is all about and make it different from another game (eg hockey). These rules cannot be changed without making it a different game;
2. rules that outline how winning is to be achieved;
3. rules that change as a result of experiencing the game and make it a better game to play.

Thus, in competing against another team or an individual we have structure that enables us to strive to win against others. But we cannot say that winning is the main point of the competition. There is only any point in striving to win if there is already value in playing the game. Also, if winning was the main point, people would seek out only those teams or individuals that they could beat and thereby achieve their objective on every occasion. But this is not the case. We attempt to win against stronger teams because of the value of striving to win and the values that we get from playing.

Young people need to understand why we have rules. Rules are framed in order to:

- provide a *structure* to enable us to play the game;
- provide *equality* when an infringement occurs to restore balance to the game;

- *protect* all players. If players wilfully violate game rules they are intentionally violating; 'the good' of all players because they elevate self-interest above the 'the good of all';
- provide a *guide to conduct*. The problems presented in a game by our opponents are obstacles to our success. It is not the players who are the obstacles. Conduct rules serve the interests of *all* players.

Thus, it is important that *all* young people learn as soon as possible that rules are essential to enjoying the satisfactions of the game. Violating these rules brings the game into disrepute and destroys the very essence of why we play games.

There is one important point that needs to be made about competition. Prior to taking part in competition, I believe it is necessary for young people to have had the opportunity to experience challenges – I call these 'personal striving challenges' – where they have recognized that they are the agents of their own personal improvement, and where success is not based on comparison with others, for example one's rank order in a race. In Chapter 5 I outline a different approach to presenting athletics in schools and this argument is developed in more detail. However, there are two points that need to be made here. The first is concerned with refocusing tasks to ensure that comparison with others is not the sole means for identifying one's success on a task. Second, young people should have the opportunity of *opting into competition* because it represents a new challenge that they wish to pursue. I make this point because it is essential that teachers consider setting developmentally appropriate competitive tasks and are sensitive to the needs of young people who find competition an overwhelming experience. There are plenty of personal striving challenges that lead young people to recognize the need for a new challenge against others.

4. LEARNING TO PREPARE FOR TAKING PART IN SPORTS EVENTS AS FESTIVALS

This feature of sport education involves a great deal of coordination because it is the central element of the whole process. Teachers have to ensure that provision is made for their pupils to acquire a practical knowledge base and put it into operation in each of the following aspects of preparation. Over the whole of a season or unit of work pupils are able to use their practical knowledge to work together as a team and prepare themselves for competition through:

(a) fitness (conditioning) over the season;
(b) developing tactics, skills and technical competence;
(c) affiliation to one's team;
(d) planning and organizing for a culminating event or festival;
(e) making plans and setting targets.

There is much to learn here and a great deal of responsibility has to be transferred to pupils to enable them to maximize their participation as an educational experience.

This organizing focus – the four sport education components – requires a different perspective because it goes beyond the teaching of techniques and the presentation of sport as a series of blocks of different sporting activities with little continuity or progression. Sport education places the learning of sporting skills in context and I believe it makes sport a much more important aspect of physical education.

At the beginning of a season or unit of work each pupil is assigned to a team in which the teacher has taken great care to ensure that they are as near equal in overall ability as possible. Over a season or unit of work on sport education the pupils will:

- practise together
- take it in turns to officiate
- elect a coach from within their team
- work out tactics
- organize their own conditioning activities
- organize their own skill practices
- take part in competitive games
- prepare as team for the festival.

At the end of the unit take part in a mini-festival.

Before the introduction of a sport education unit it may be appropriate to use two or three other units to develop the model and to provide pupils with the practical knowledge base to organize their own unit. It is important to stress that each lesson should establish a model that provides a structure of things that need to be covered. Each lesson may have specific sections to highlight the key features of sport education. In this way, pupils acquire a way of working that can be transferred to their own planning.

Some pupils may find it helpful if the teacher can provide cue cards that provide a range of ideas on:

- officiating
- technique and skill practices
- tactical dimensions
- conditioning practices
- appropriate behaviour in competitions.

These can be colour-coded to indicate level of difficulty. Fair Play Awards can be instigated and criteria determined in consultation with pupils.

AT WHAT AGE SHOULD WE INTRODUCE SPORT EDUCATION?

Sport as a disciplined form of physical activity needs to be represented to young people in a form that is acceptable to their level of understanding and maturity. This is important because I am not advocating that we introduce sport as a disciplined form to very young children. It is much more important to recognize that sport can be translated into a play form that makes it much more developmentally appropriate to children at Key Stages 1 and 2. Thus, I am proposing that 'Sport as play' and 'Sport as a disciplined activity', although closely interrelated, need to be acknowledged as mutually separate, independent aspects of sport that require different approaches and challenges.

I would argue that we need to consider two phases:

Phase 1: ages 9–13   Phase 2: ages 14–18

In Phase 1 I would propose that in a sports education curriculum we should include the following:

1. *Cultural sports* these represent playground games or physical activities that children used to play during school breaks or lunch periods but that appear to be vanishing from our playgrounds. It could be an important aspect of the school physical

43

education curriculum to reintroduce them and encourage young people to play them at home.

2. *Games-making or inventing games* these represent important opportunities for young people to be inventive and develop their own unique school book of invented games, which can be used in competitions. In addition, they provide opportunities for young people to learn about rules (structure, equality, protection and safety, and conduct) and their role in the development of a game.

3. *Students of sport* sports can become absorbing interests as pupils start collecting information about a sport, a team or a sports personality. Young people can learn a great deal and learn to value and care deeply about a sport.

4. *Sporting challenges* one of the main roles of a teacher is to stimulate further participation beyond the school and to recognize all young people's participation efforts. The exercise challenge has promoted participation in healthy physical activities, and it may be appropriate to examine how this model can be applied to sport. The notion of a Challenge Curriculum, outlined in Chapter 1, encompasses a whole range of individual and team sports, entailing participation, can-do and creative challenges.

These four aspects represent additional features of sport that we can promote together with a concern for organizing sport education as preparation for a festival.

I am convinced that sport education in the form of preparing for a festival can work well because of two instances I have observed. A group of over 20 primary school boys formed their own football league, selected small-sided teams, organized their own training sessions and arranged for neutral referees (or did it themselves at certain games) and went to car-boot sales to find trophies. This went on for about ten weeks in the summer. In the second instance my twins (12 years old) go to school early in the morning to play a series of fixtures against other teams. It is well organized with a fixtures list and trophies that they have made; transfer deals are even conducted. It has attracted a large group of boys and three girls. This is entirely pupil-organized and no help from adults has been sought.

During Phase 1 the role of modification principles needs to be highlighted. Even though modification ideas have been around for some considerable time there has been little documentation about how this can be achieved. The mini-game has spawned some ideas and though this represents only one approach, some sport governing bodies are extending it to outline other possibilities. This needs to be encouraged. Here I am suggesting that we consider modification in terms of content, learning and task:

1. Modification of content – representation of adult games through enabling games by modifying:
- technical demands
- tactics through exaggeration (see Chapter 4)
- complexity of tactics – some games need to be taught first.
2. Modification of learning:
- developmentally appropriate activities
- modification of playing area, targets rules, size of teams, scoring system for safety reasons (see Ellis, 1986).
3. Modification of the task – so that all pupils can answer the task:
- differentiation, eg some pupils/students need different starting points and may pursue different routes
- changing the focus of the task, eg in athletics the three-second run (see Chapter 5).

In Phase 2 we may need to consider that sport education can be pursued through three quite distinct routes:

Route 1: participation in a range of sports leading to a festival. This aspect represents the practical element of sport education in the selection of sports that a teacher uses to illustrate the model.

Route 2: sport as a vocational route in order to gain recognized qualifications as an official or coach (or leader). There are a number of recognized qualifications leading to an award for coaching (or leadership) and officiating that can be developed for students at Key Stage 4 (KS4) (14–16). These can be part of a vocational focused course as well as the practical element of sport education.

Route 3: sport education as a form of 'badge of academic merit'; in other words, a formal examination course in which students are assessed for GCSE or A-level. There are good reasons why sport education should be seen as an academic course with practical components. In many cases this would expand and develop the idea of sport education and give real focus to the academic course.

45

Sport education could also involve the following:

Students learning to organize their own club. Some teachers exclude an activity from the curriculum because there are no avenues to pursue it when students leave school. This seems like a golden opportunity to develop the idea that courses need to be provided that teach students how to form, organize and run their own club (including financial concerns). There is a lot to learn and this aspect of sport education could represent a significant development.

A *school sports council organized by the students.* If sport education is going to develop it needs to be seen as a collaborative venture between students and staff. By setting up a school sports council to organize and run extracurricular sport (the extended curriculum) we can expand the idea of sport education and reinforce important educational and sporting aspirations. Once again such ideas need to be spelled out in greater detail. In the late 1960s I developed such a scheme in my own school and though it took five years to mature into a reasonably successful model, I believe it showed that there is a great deal of potential in developing the idea.

SPORT EDUCATION AND FAIR PLAY

One of the most important aspects of sport education is its association with fair play. This is a particularly important element that needs further elaboration, so I propose to devote a major part of this chapter to a consideration of its relevance to sport education.

What does fair play involve? It is concerned with:

- not breaking rules deliberately
- not seeking to gain unfair advantages
- not exploiting situations for one's selfish desire
- not taking unacceptable actions (eg, intimidation; direct aggression; verbal abuse; disagreements with officials or anyone in authority).

It is easier to understand the motivating power of fair play if it is seen as something that a young person should want to do in order to make the game better, rather than as something he or she is unwillingly constrained to do. If we are going to promote fair play and generate positive attitudes in the game, we need to look at the responsibilities of the player, the teacher and parents. We can accomplish this by identifying and listing behaviours we feel are unacceptable and those that we wish to promote. This list of negative and positive principles can become a checklist for examining the behaviour of our pupils.

In the same way, teachers need to consider their own actions and explore whether they promote fair play and positive attitudes towards others and the game. Young people need consistent messages and to feel safe and secure in the routines that teachers establish. With a commitment from the teacher, young people can learn a great deal about fair play and acquire positive attitudes in a context that highlights and reinforces key fair play principles. Because they represent powerful influences, teachers should be aware of their behaviour and actions, the language they use and the relationships they establish with young people. If we are to promote fair play then teachers need to allocate time during training sessions to highlight and reinforce key messages and behaviour. In the same way that they practise skills and tactics, young people need the opportunity to practise fair play.

Thus it is essential that we examine what kind of things teachers should promote and what things they should refrain from doing. This can be achieved in the same way as with pupils. Teachers can construct a list of negative and positive principles that they believe influence fair play and positive attitudes.

In addition, teachers need to remember that they are role models to all their players and therefore they represent once again a powerful agent for influencing the behaviour of young people, particularly towards officials. Thus, avoid blaming officials for the short-comings of a team or player; teach them life is full of close calls and subjective decisions. The next time you have the desire to yell at a referee, try to say something positive. If you hear parents or other spectators decrying the eyesight of the referee, disagree and point out that he or she is doing the right thing.

Teach all your players that rules are mutual agreements to create a good game. Keep in mind, at all times, that the chief objectives of playing a sport are to have fun, learn skills and build self-confidence. Your primary purpose is not to produce a star, however important you believe it to be. Your challenge is to make sport so much fun that your pupils want to be involved and keep coming back for more.

A teacher needs to establish housekeeping rules that make life easier for players when they win or lose. Before a game some young people may be stressed, anxious and possibly frightened that they will let you (the teacher) down or their team players or their parents. The teacher needs to develop strategies to support them.

If we measure a season only by the number of wins or losses we underplay a whole range of indicators of success that your players may value. We might be able to generate a winning season for all by highlighting personal performance rather than just results of games. In other words, we need to adopt strategies that allow individuals to measure their own success and feel satisfaction with their efforts: successes that can be recognized by others – team players, parents and teachers.

Finally, it is essential to recognize that all young people need self-discipline (or control) and empathy with their teacher and other players. Without these, it is difficult to establish an ethos that promotes fair play for all and positive attitudes towards fellow players and opponents.

In a teacher's endeavours to promote fair play and positive attitudes, it may be appropriate to enlist the support of parents whose children are playing for a school team. This can be reinforced by sending out a letter to parents; which could include the following:

- The team's goals for the season and what you value (compliment each other, accept officials' decisions, etc).
- Team policies (attendance and opportunities for all players to be involved in games).
- Typical procedures during training sessions and matches.
- What can be expected of the teacher.
- What the teacher expects of each player.
- How parents can help the team (including encouraging playing fairly and respecting each other). If we can get parents to support the teacher's attempt to promote fair play, youth sport will benefit and it will have cleared a major hurdle.

It may well be appropriate to invite parents to a meeting at the beginning of the season and explain that the team is highlighting the value of fair play and seeking parents' support on the touch line and in their interactions with their own children and their friends. A code of conduct for parents may be presented.

You may well want to answer the following questions about your views on teaching and fair play.

- What do I want from teaching these young people to play sport? Winning, gaining recognition, assisting in the development a young person's potential, helping them to learn all about soccer?
- What are the needs of these young people in my care?
- Are they taking part for fun, to meet friends or make new ones, develop their soccer skills, or win games?
- How can my teaching meet the needs of the young person?
- Do I value fair play? Do I care more about winning and losing than right and wrong?
- In my teaching does my behaviour encourage positive attitudes towards other players; does it reinforce fair play by everyone? Am I a consistent role model? Do I set a good example?
- What is my stance on respecting rules and officials? Do I encourage young players to treat officials with respect and accept their decisions?
- What are my responsibilities to opposing teachers and players? Am I a consistent and exemplary role model?
- What would I like to accomplish by the end of the season? Do I want my players to become cooperative and value playing fairly?
- How can I accomplish my goals?

ATTITUDES THAT REINFORCE FAIR PLAY PRINCIPLES

So far I have highlighted fair play principles but they are underpinned and supported by a variety of attitudes. Therefore, it is important to examine these in more detail to understand something of their significance.

Young people acquire a number of very different attitudes. In particular, they acquire attitudes towards themselves that are influenced a great deal by other people in their lives, especially significant others like teachers, their own team players and parents. Thus, the language that people use, the signals that they give out and their actions are important indications of how we value others. The messages that young people receive from these interactions and messages influence how they view themselves, their potential as a player, their progress and their achievements. Also, if their aspirations are rewarded when their efforts bring clear indications of progress and they *recognize* that they are improving, young people will begin to formulate a positive

49

image of themselves. Thus, it is important that all teachers recognize the need to identify indicators of progress that allow all young people in their care to acquire positive images and enable them to believe in themselves.

One's attitudes towards other team members is dependent upon positive relationships that are reciprocated, a feeling that everyone is working together and that cooperation is mutually valued. Respect has to be earned, however, so it is essential that all team members recognize that they need to cooperate and help each other to get better.

Attitudes towards the opposition should centre on the belief that they are worthy opponents because they will present us with difficult problems that we will have to strive hard to overcome in order to win the game. As worthy opponents we need to respect their capabilities, be generous in our praise of their efforts and see playing as a mutual quest to create a good game. Young people need to learn a series of rituals in which compliments can be made and congratulations can be given willingly.

Our attitudes towards the referee or any official must be governed by a recognition of their role as a guardian of the rules, not simply as an enforcer of the rules, and also as an instrument for making a good game. All players have responsibilities to abide by the rules of the game and the spirit of their sport and to assist the referee whenever possible. This means that in difficult decisions young people need to learn to acknowledge any infringement on their part and not to rely wholly on the referee to interpret what happened. The decisions of referees should be accepted without question or protest. Players have to recognize that referees have a difficult job to do and mistakes can be made, so there is a need to exercise self-control at all times.

A player acquires attitudes about their teacher. Such attitudes are dependent on the interactions, the language and the messages that teachers give out to young people. In the same way that all young people should respect the decisions of referees, they should recognize that teachers are trying to be fair, generous in their praise, considerate and attentive. Teachers can reinforce positive attitudes towards themselves by remembering that children find it hard to understand negative instructions and easier to understand positive reinforcement. Only use justified praise: young people are quick to recognize when you don't really mean it and it loses its significance. Therefore, after a game or practice session have something positive to say to everyone – talk to *all* team players. Thank them for their efforts and for playing fair. Children need recognition and will respond to it with very positive attitudes towards their teacher.

Finally, fair play is bound up with young people's progress in the game. If a teacher can accomplish it, fair play will not be an option, it will be a central commitment of all players, teachers and officials.

REFERENCES

Alderson, G J K (1982) *Thinking About the PE Curriculum*, report of the 2nd Annual Conference of Heads of Departments in Post-Primary Schools, Ballymena, Co. Antrim: North Eastern Educational and Library Board, pp. 2–31.

Alderson, G J K and Critchley, D (1990) 'Physical education and the National Curriculum' in *New Directions in Physical Education vol.1*, N Armstrong (ed.), Champaign, Ill.: Human Kinetics, pp.37–62.

Alexander, K R and Taggart, A (1995) *The Sport Education in Physical Education Program*, Canberra: Australian Government Publishing Service.

Arnold, P (1979) *Meaning in Movement, Sport and Physical Education*, Oxford: Heinemann.

Best, D (1978) *Philosophy and Human Movement*, London: Allen & Unwin.

Ellis, M (1986) 'Modification of games' in *Rethinking Games Teaching*, R Thorpe, D Bunker and L Almond (eds), Loughborough: Esmond Publications, pp.75–7.

Grant, B, Sharp, P and Siedentop, D (1992) *Sport Education in Physical Education: A Teacher's Guide*, Wellington: Hilary Commission.

Siedentop, D (1994) *Sport Education: Quality PE Through Positive Sport Experiences*, Champaign, Ill.: Human Kinetics.

CHAPTER FOUR

A changing focus in games teaching

Rod Thorpe and David Bunker

INTRODUCTION

Throughout the 1970s an approach to teaching games was formulated that placed the emphasis on ensuring that children understood the games they played while capitalizing on the intrinsic motivation most youngsters bring to playing the game. It is interesting to note that we use the phrase 'playing the game' but we do not use the phrases 'playing athletics' or 'playing swimming'. The problem seems to have been that a number of teachers found it difficult to resolve the relationship between the game and game skills.

Clearly to play a game well the skills have to be well practised and it is logical to give children as much skill practice as possible. The major problem with this approach is that we (and many teachers, we discovered later) realized that for many children the time available in the curriculum was insufficient to perfect or even reach adequate levels with many of the games skills, particularly if the teacher was always teaching the average child. The less able were forced to recognize their inadequacies and the very able went unchallenged. The whole class waited for the game, particularly in those lessons based on the quite common format of an introduction and a technique/skill, followed by a game. Of course, teachers taught through the game and conditioned practices but by their own admission did not really have a clear philosophy or framework within which to work. This problem seems to be international, if the comment made in the introduction to our article, presented in the *South Australian PE Bulletin* in 1984, is typical:

> the idea of progressing from tactics to skills, or from Why? to How? rather than vice versa, is not new, but its organisation and application has not previously been made coherent.

The interchange with students, teachers, advisers and our colleagues led us to propose a model that was first published in the *Bulletin of Physical Education* (1982). The model, shown in Figure 4.1, is central to the way we plan lessons and/or units of work and indeed helps us to formulate an overall programme. It is included here by way of introduction.

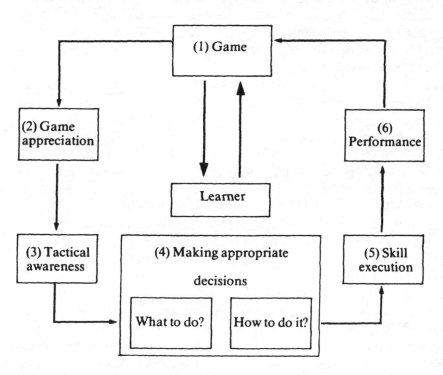

Figure 4.1 Model for games teaching

It is important to recognize that while the approach stresses understanding, that understanding is incomplete if it is not done in the practical situation. The overt sign that understanding has been fully gained is some form of appropriate response.

It may be idealistic (and why not?) to hope that we can educate future generations who can watch games on the television and understand the basic tactics involved.

Thorpe *et al*. (1986) have discussed the idea that we can develop a games curriculum based on this model coupled with four fundamentals:

- sampling;
- modification – representation;
- modification – exaggeration;
- tactical complexity.

In our experience the person who really understands the game of soccer can appreciate what players are trying to do in a hockey game and is certainly not completely unaware of basketball tactics. If fundamental principles have been stressed and understood, Australian rules, American football and rugby fall into place. One initial role of the games teacher is to determine the games to teach to ensure a sound base from which the children can view other games. Clearly, a number of games must be taught to reflect the variety that exists but equally if we expect children to develop an understanding of a particular game we must allow them sufficient time to do so. We are forced to 'sample' from the range of games available to us, not only for the variety of experiences but recognizing that 'possibilities exist that can show similarities between apparently dissimilar games and differences between apparently similar games, all leading to a much better understanding of games in general' (Thorpe *et al*., 1986, p.164).

The division of modification into two fundamentals is not mere semantics – teachers can modify a game so that it 'represents' as closely as possible the adult game. This usually means that the tactical intricacies are still retained, that is the attraction. These 'mini-games' are a 'representation' of the major game in a form suitable for children (modified equipment, reduced numbers) and allow them to associate with the adult model. What they do not always do is pose tactical problems that, with some thought and practice, can be 'solved' by children. For this to happen elements of the games have to be exaggerated. A 'thin' badminton court that makes it obvious that the space to attack is at the front and back of the court is an example of exaggeration.

If the aim is to ensure that children understand the games they play it would seem logical to start with the simpler games. In fact, we find 11-a-side soccer being taught to 9 year-olds while the tactically less complex game of 1 *v* 1 badminton or tennis is left until 14 years of age. With the development of modified games and the availability of sufficient equipment it becomes far more realistic to present the tactically simple games first, which would seem to be a sensible procedure.

These four fundamentals will be used to develop a 5–16 curriculum, because they provide a framework of principles to guide our practice.

GAMES IN THE PRIMARY SCHOOL

It is of course ironic that while most physical education specialists recognize that the 5–11 year period is vital for physical development few specialists work in this area. This has often resulted in a very limited games experience in the primary school. It might be useful to consider four approaches to games that are or could be seen in the primary school.

First, the physical education lesson consists of movement, gymnastics, dance, or relays, and the children have a separate games lesson in which they play seven-a-side netball, 11-a-side soccer and, when it is warm, nine-a-side rounders with the teacher as the feeder. Of course we feel that this is quite inappropriate: the children get few chances to use skills learnt and there is little chance of children understanding the games they play.

Second, the physical education lesson is as above but when it comes to the games, teachers use 'mini' forms of the adult game eg, 4 *v* 4 netball with players allowed to go anywhere on their court except that only the two attackers can go in the other team's semi-circle and only the two defenders can go in their own semi-circle. A general agreement that all primary schools will play mini-games in lessons and in school matches would improve the games experience dramatically. Selecting one or two 'mini' invasion games such as 4 *v* 4 netball or 5 *v* 5 soccer/rugby/hockey, a court game or two (eg, 3 *v* 3 volleyball or short tennis) or a small sided fielding game like 5 *v* 5 rounders or cricket, would ensure a more varied and more valuable game experience (we think). Even so we are not convinced that the problems set by these games are clear enough for the children to find solutions to them.

Third, it can be argued that traditional games have been developed for adults by adults and that merely reducing them to 'mini games' is still not moving far enough if children are to really understand. It may be far better to choose and/or design games specifically to suit children at this stage of their learning and development.

Fourth, the recognition that games should be designed for children leads quite naturally to the idea that children can be allowed to design and develop their own games within confines set by the teacher. The area of games–making, particularly when used with a well structured programme and not as an excuse for the teacher's failure to think about games, can help children to understand the need for rules and simple tactics.

Finally, if one believes that the underlying central theme of games education is to build up an understanding of how to play games, it goes without saying that whatever games are selected they should be arranged in an order that allows the development of this understanding. It may be necessary to move from one set of games to another if this is to be achieved.

FOR PRIMARY SCHOOL INFANTS (5–7)

A pupil throws the ball somewhere specific – a simple target game occurs – 'Can I hit that "object"?'

A friend joins in and we start to count – 'I'll have five goes, then you have five goes', 'How many did we get together?', 'I beat you'. At this stage we may start to help children to 'compete' with care.

The teacher encourages the children to aim for different sorts of target, a hoop on the floor, a circle on the wall, a bucket, etc.

The partner becomes a target who has to catch the ball without moving. Here, we are still playing target games.

FOR JUNIORS (7–11)

One throws the ball at a big target – the other tries to stop it hitting the target. The target on the wall might now look like a goal. The target on the floor might now be a court. The children learn to throw away from the goalkeeper or fielder, who finds out how to defend the area (Figure 4.2).

Figure 4.2   Children bowling towards and defending a target

From this point we could let two children work together to defend the area against the thrower; now they are involved in a fielding game.

Having ensured that the children are now clear on how to attack a space and how to defend it, they can be moved to alternate rapidly between attack and defence by playing a divided court game (Figure 4.3).

With two squares an appropriate distance apart and perhaps a large sponge ball, we can play throw catch tennis or badminton.

Putting a high net between the two courts and introducing another two players we can move from 1 *v* 1 towards a 2 *v* 2 throw volleyball-type game.

Put the net away, put the children into threes, each three in their own square, and play 'piggy in the middle'; the piggy is like the net but of course she or he can move – we have taken the first step towards 4 *v* 4 invasion games mentioned previously.

At any stage the teacher can move off into a more recognizable game, eg, 1 *v* 1 throw tennis becomes 1 *v* 1 short tennis if a bat is used, but perhaps only after the 2 *v* 2 fielding game so that the youngsters get used to using the bat with a friend feeding them.

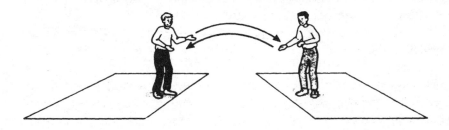

Figure 4.3   Alternate attacking and defending

For us the ideal primary games programme would lead children through games that become increasingly complex, leaning heavily on throw-catch games at first that allow the children to catch, hold and look: they often need that time to think.

THE FOUNDATION COURSE

The primary school physical education experience for most children will have been limited to playing invasion games, which are without doubt the most difficult games to play. Whether it be on a scaled-down football pitch or on a small size netball court, the skills involved in receiving the ball, controlling it and directing the pass, with an opponent, sometimes more than one, breathing down the neck, are much too demanding for all but a very few. In the light of their 'poor skills' some children find themselves practising 'ball skills' in the first year of their secondary school games course. While such courses may be of some help, it is inevitable that much of the work is based on techniques with next to no time spent on playing games. We see little justification for this and strongly recommend that a game-centred course be taught in the first year that lays a firm foundation for what is to follow. If the games chosen create interest and strong motivation, the skills will be practised and performance will improve. It could be that one of the major reasons why children can't throw is because they don't throw.

In presenting a foundation course we would suggest that teachers start a 2 v 2 striking–fielding game. The more controlled tempo within such games can be a real advantage: the striker is free to choose when and where to hit the ball and need not be too concerned with what happens next. The ball will not come straight back form the other side and nobody is going to get close enough to interfere with the strike. To get the striking–fielding game going we need to change the bat and ball and make sure that the striker and pitcher – becoming a cooperative feeder – are on the same side. In so doing skill thresholds are reduced and we stand a much better chance of keeping players, particularly the fielders, more involved. It should be said that there is no place in such a foundation course for the 'traditional' games of rounders or cricket... elsewhere maybe.

A 2 v 2 game can be played quite conveniently on an area the size of a badminton court. The fielders defend half the court while the strike is

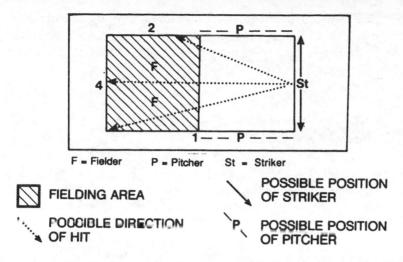

F = Fielder   P = Pitcher   St = Striker

▨ FIELDING AREA

POSSIBLE POSITION OF STRIKER

POSSIBLE DIRECTION OF HIT

P POSSIBLE POSITION OF PITCHER

Figure 4.4   2 v 2 game showing striking and defending areas

made form anywhere behind the baseline. This is shown in Figure 4.4.

The striker can choose whether to self-feed or to receive a 'friendly' throw from the pitcher. Any striking implement can be used and any kind of soft ball, a padder bat and a sponge tennis ball make an interesting combination. In the early stages some youngsters should be allowed to throw the ball into the fielding area if they so wish. To complete an innings both players have six hits each – one point is given if the ball crosses the line at halfway, two for the sidelines and four for the backline but the ball *must bounce* in the fielding area.

A good deal of teaching material stems form this simple game situation. Particular lessons might take account of the following points:

- How is the striker coming to terms with the problem of making the ball bounce in the fielding area? Is she or he hitting from high to low? or bending down to hit a 'skimmer', or sending the ball along the floor? Is the ball being hit hard or being placed into an open space? Is there any use of spin, angles and disguise?
- Where do the fielders take up position at the start of the game? Are they standing side-by-side, at front or back, or are they fielding one behind the other? Why do they field in these positions? Which fielder takes responsibility for the space down the middle? What is the most effective way of stopping the ball?

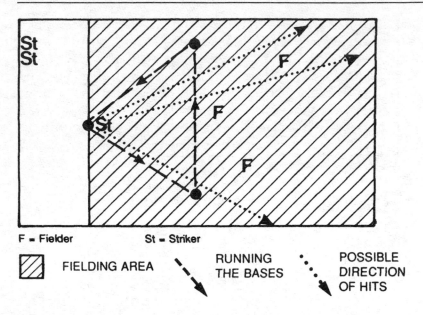

F = Fielder   St = Striker

▨ FIELDING AREA   RUNNING
THE BASES   POSSIBLE
DIRECTION
OF HITS

Figure 4.5   3 v 3 game using more than one ball

Over the last few years we have built a basic 3 *v* 3 game into our work on a foundation course. The format of the game is quite different from the 2 *v* 2 set up, the striker is confronted with an unusual task and much more is asked of the fielders (Figure 4.5).

The striker hits three balls, one after the other (or simultaneously) into the fielding area and then runs round the bases (of course there is no reason why the balls should not be thrown or kicked into the fielding area). Meanwhile the fielders retrieve the balls and return them as quickly as possible to any two of the bases before the striker completes the 'home run'. Points can be awarded for reaching first and second bases.

The striker must decide when, where and how to hit the balls. Is it best to launch them in rapid fire, or to delay the third hit momentarily? Should the hits be directed at any one fielder? Might it be a good idea to play all three balls into the close field or should they be hit high and deep into the back field?

With so many options available to the striker, the fielders will have plenty to think about. First and foremost they will have to work as a team. Where should the field be set? Is it better for two fielders to cover the deep field? Who is going to receive the ball on the bases? Should one of the fielders run one ball to a base instead of throwing it? Planning for every eventuality is going to take some time!

Too often we see striking–fielding games being played in which there is too little activity. After waiting some time for a hit, few youngsters make a good contact (or any contact) with the ball, which, in turn, means that the fielders are made redundant. This should not be allowed to happen in the foundation course, or, we would add, in later years.

The following is but one example of a game that keeps everyone on their toes and that requires those taking part, especially the fielders, to think about the tactics use (Figure 4.6).

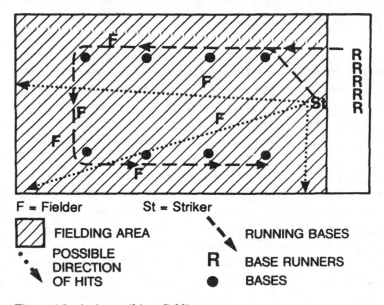

F = Fielder   St = Striker

▨ FIELDING AREA   RUNNING BASES

• POSSIBLE DIRECTION OF HITS   **R** BASE RUNNERS

● BASES

Figure 4.6 Active striking–fielding game

The game starts with a self-feed and a strike into the fielding area. One of the fielders recovers the ball and sends it to base 1 from where it is transferred round the bases to finish at base 8. As soon as the hit is made, the striker sets off closely followed by others in the team, to complete a run round the bases. The fact that everyone on the striking side runs the bases after every hit makes this a demanding game for them as well as the fielders. The game gives plenty of scope for introducing different scoring systems. The tactics developed in response to changes in the scoring will give an indication of the understanding of the different games being played. Whatever else may happen, the striker will have to decide where best to hit the ball – 'as far away from the first base as possible' – a good tactic if the rule states that the ball must be relayed from first base… and the fielders will have to come together to decide on their individual responsibilities for retrieving the ball and covering the bases as well as the best means of transforming the ball from base to base – it could depend on the type of ball being used.

It does not take much to step out of a fielding game into a court game. The 2 v 2 striking–fielding game only requires a barrier to be set up to separate the two teams and we have all the makings of a court game. The barrier, whether it be a line, a space or a net, prevents one player from invading the other's territory and allows a hit to be made in relative comfort. However, in such games, it is probable that there will be little time to recover before the ball comes back from the other side. Because of this, much of the work in the early stages of teaching court games explores throw–catch situations. It is important that a rally takes place for only then is it possible to further a youngster's games education on court. The following games presented sequentially in terms of their increasing difficulty, largely determined by the time available for the return, draw attention to the dos (and don'ts) of court games:

1. Throw-catch (1 v 1) a large foam ball over a high net that divides a long, thin court. The ball must bounce once before the catch. With a slow ball and a high net, the rallies are long; there is plenty of time to execute the throw.
   Points to note. The importance of throwing to the baseline to keep the opponent as far away from the net as possible. It is much easier to win the point from close to the net.

2. The same 1v 1 game but with a rule change: the ball must not bounce.
   Points to note. Continue to throw long, wait for an opportunity to win the point, ie your opponent is out of position at the back of the court. Drop the ball over the net into the space at the front of the court.

3. Add another rule to the same 1 v 1 game: the ball must be thrown form the catch position.
   Points to note. Make every effort to catch the ball at its highest point; throwing from below the height of the net will give both

the time and the opportunity for your opponent to make a winning return. Remember that to throw (or hit) from low to high is to defend. After each throw recover quickly to the point on the court that helps you defend the court.

4. A 2 *v* 2 passing game introduces the element of team play and could bring the hit into the game: one of the players, after making a catch, throws the ball for the other to hit over the net. It is a good idea to let the second player decide on whether to catch and throw or whether to hit over the net. To keep the rally going, the advantage to be gained from the hits on one side of the net is offset by allowing the ball to bounce once on the other side.
Points to note. The first catcher takes aim to make sure that the ball is 'set' high in the front court, near to the net. The other player prepares to hit or throw down into the opponents' court.

From here a 3 *v* 3 game requiring a catch-throw, a throw, and a hit from both teams is not far removed from the 'dig', 'set' and 'spike' sequence of the game of volleyball.

With some idea as to how to play a good tactical game and with some experience of hitting the ball, albeit with the hand, we might now introduce a padder bat and a small, slow ball to facilitate the 'hit–hit' sequence of the more traditional court games. In retaining the one bounce rule and a high net, it is hoped that rallies will develop and that many, if not all, of the points made in the throw–catch games will be transferred to this modified game of padder tennis. As things improve, ie the rallies become more prolonged, other changes, notably lowering the net, bringing the volley into play, introducing a short tennis racket, can be made.

At the end of the foundation course on court games, it would be most reassuring to watch rallies in which deep approach shots were opening up the court for winning vollies. It would be even more reassuring to see a good approach shot met with an equally good defensive lob, a recovery to make another approach shot to force a more shallow lob and a winning smash. It is clear that each shot is being played to good purpose and shows a well developed tactical understanding of the changing circumstances of the rally.

We would start our work in the invasion games by playing 'pig in the middle', a game well known to 11-year-olds. The 2 *v* 1 situation is fundamental in the teaching of invasion games. An instruction to 'keep the ball for 30 seconds' (keepball) might result in the youngster with the ball doing very little except hold on to it! Great!... but the defender might not allow this to happen if a decision is made to attack the ball. But now the defender has been drawn towards the ball, space has been created and the pass can be made more safely. In getting the receiver to take up good positions, some time (and not a little effort) will be necessary to establish the need to move off the ball, to move away from the ball more often, perhaps, than towards it, to change direction and to provide the best possible passing angle.

Another instruction 'to make as many passes as possible in 30 seconds' (speedball) puts a much greater burden on the receiver. A thinking defender will mark one player only who when passing and receiving will find it difficult to create space, but does it matter if the pass is not made as long as the ball can be recovered quickly for another attempt? However, if a penalty of three points is incurred for an incomplete pass it would make the player in possession think twice before releasing the ball. The risk might be too great; if so the ball will be held to wait for a better passing opportunity.

The calculation of risk and safety in attacking (and defending) a variety of targets, some stationary, others moving, some wide, some narrow, is fundamental to an appreciation and understanding of invasion games. The juxtaposition of the two games 'keepball' (30 seconds) and 'speedball' (many passes) shows quite clearly how a simple rule change alters the game quite dramatically and causes the thinking player to respond differently to the task.

In developing the work further, we have tended to introduce a game along the lines of skittleball. At first few rules are prescribed – as youngsters see the need for a rule it can be incorporated into the game – usually a passing game emerges in which there is no contact, a 'no-go' area around the target, no travelling and no running with the ball. Points are scored for hitting the skittle. How are we going to make our attack? We must move the ball quickly to the target; if an interception is made it might be worth the risk to take a long shot to penetrate to the target.

The defence might try to guard against the 'fast break' by making sure that one player delays the pass or shot by attacking the ball carrier while the others recover to concentrate (or zone) around the skittle. On the other hand, defenders might decide to mark one-for-one to increase the likelihood of regaining possession quickly and to keep the opposition penned in their own half. Decisions such as this must be explored through principles of play and taken in the context of the rules for the game.

For some time (and long before American football became popular in this country) we have played a game that we call 'lineball' to contrast with 'skittleball'. Instead of playing on a long narrow pitch the game is played across so that the 'end' line being attacked is wide (in marked contrast to the narrow goal of skittleball). A score is made by either running with the ball in possession over the line into a large 'end' zone or by throwing the ball into this end zone to be received by a team-mate.

A run comes to a halt if a defender manages to tag the runner – the ball must now be thrown with the possibility that possession may be lost (notice that possession is not surrendered despite the tag). This rule is intended to encourage youngsters to run forward with the ball. Very few of them, given their first taste of rugby football, make a forward move. Once they are forced into passing backwards the ball usually finishes behind their own goal line.

In giving all the advantages to the attacking team, the defenders must feed off the scraps. The intended receiver may drop the ball, the defender may knock the ball away or better still make an interception; if so, the pass is incomplete and the defending team wins possession. The defenders will need some time to work out the most effective way to protect their line – some form of one-on-one marking will be necessary to stop the run, hopefully before it starts.

It might pay dividends to leave one player at least to mark space in a 5 v 5 game. It might be the right thing to do if one team has more players than another but we do not know for certain. The important thing is to find out what works, when it works and why it works. And, of course, while this is going on, we take every opportunity to draw attention to what was covered in 2 v 1, 3 v 1 situations – drawing an opponent, disguising the pass, making an angle, calculating the risks, etc.

You cannot spend too much time in planning the foundation course because it is fundamental to a games education and it contains the building blocks for later work in the recognized games.

As part of the foundation course, 'games making' , started in the primary school, should be continued and some of the ideas gleaned from children's games will contain many of the ingredients of the 'real' game and, as such, will require that some time be given to find ways round the problems that the game presents. If we teach games, with understanding as a clear objective, supported by the content suggested, the foundation course might capture the interest of a large majority of the youngsters in their first year of the PE curriculum.

FROM THE FOUNDATION COURSE TO A SPECIFIC GAME

CRICKET

In making the move from the foundation course into a more 'recognized' game, it is helpful to refer to the 2 v 2 fielding game described previously. With a padder bat, the striker directs the hit towards a predetermined target area having been 'fed' by a cooperative server. The fielder's plan their tactics, make decisions on the positions to take up, adjust the positions if necessary, work out the angles and hopefully, stop the ball. It is but a short step into a game that looks a little like cricket. With a cricket bat and tennis ball now to hand, the striker (batter) faces the cooperative feeder (bowler) to receive a throw that allows for a good, strong hit to a target area on the 'leg-side' of the striker (Figure 4.7).

The feeder and striker must work together to find the sort of delivery that can be despatched most easily to the target (fielding) area. It should not be too long before most 12/13-year-olds come up with the answer: a ball, bouncing about half-way, aimed at the body and arriving at waist height... the bounce gives time to prepare for the shot that is made at a comfortable height. But what sort of shot? Let them work it out. It would be surprising if most youngsters were not playing something akin to the 'pull shot' after some trial-and-error practice. A good contact should be well rewarded as this is a strong hitting action using muscles of the legs and trunk as well as long arms... and worth the risk of using a striking surface no more than 4¼ in deep. Including a rule that requires the batter to hit the ball down on to the ground in the fielding area before a run can be scored demands that the pull shot is played from high to low, the more so if it has been decided to reward the fielders for taking a catch. A relocation and slight readjustment to the target area presents a different set of problems for the players involved. This is illustrated in Figure 4.8.

Again we should ask, 'what is the best way to feed the ball for the striker to hit into the fielding area?' and again we should set time aside for discussion, negotiation and decision. It is possible that a 'full toss'

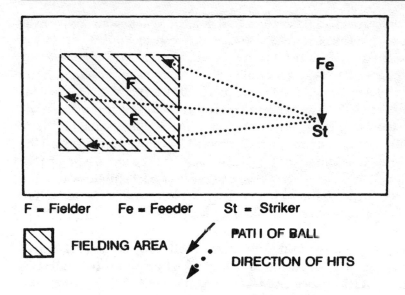

F = Fielder   Fe = Feeder   St = Striker

FIELDING AREA   PATH OF BALL

DIRECTION OF HITS

Figure 4.7   Fielding game starting to resemble cricket

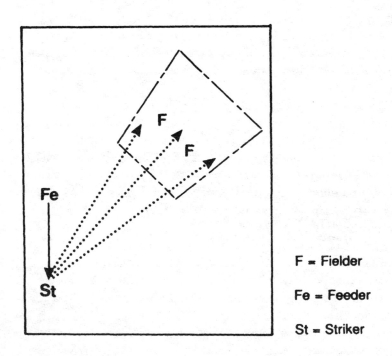

F = Fielder

Fe = Feeder

St = Striker

Figure 4.8   Consequences of altering target area

may be the answer or a throw-feed that bounces twice before arriving. It is also possible that the throw will be directed to the 'offside' of the striker to make it easier to hit into the fielding area. As youngsters find out the best ways to feed we should be taking notes of the shape of the shot that is being produced. Some may favour hitting with a horizontal bat, quite naturally so, but this may create difficulties on account of the rotational forces at work, while others may be keeping the bat in a more vertical plane. As we know, this will increase the chances of sending the ball in the required direction as the full length of the bat is being put to the ball – deliveries that arrive close to the ground, ie full toss and half volley are difficult to hit with a horizontal bat. (It might be as well to point out for future reference that the vertical bat protects much more of the 'wicket' than the horizontal one.)

Many teachers and coaches of cricket will have noticed how close these 'games' are to the drills they present after initial teaching of a particular shot and before its use in the game. But we always start with a game that challenges the youngster to search for an appropriate shot, and then we might want to give some technical information to the batter in the production of the pull to leg or the drive to off. Comments such as 'keep the head still', 'weight over the ball' are fundamental, helpful and probably sufficient, particularly if the rule of being caught is part of the game. It should be remembered that technical advice is given only when it is needed and it is always appropriate to the individual concerned.

So far little has been said about the fielders; of course, every opportunity will have been taken to reinforce material from the foundation course, but it is a fact that they are dependent upon what is happening between the bowler and the batter, with the bowler feeding accurately and the batter striking consistently and with the purpose of penetrating the field, the fielders come more into the picture. The game shown in Figure 4.9 brings them to the centre of the stage.

The rules might be:

- no runs scored unless the ball is hit into the fielding area;
- the ball must be kept below head height for runs to be scored;
- the batter scores 'one', 'two', or 'four' if the ball crosses the appropriate boundary line;
- two bonus runs are scored if the batter completes a 'run' between the wickets; and
- the batter is penalized, eg, loses a life, loses runs, if 'caught' or

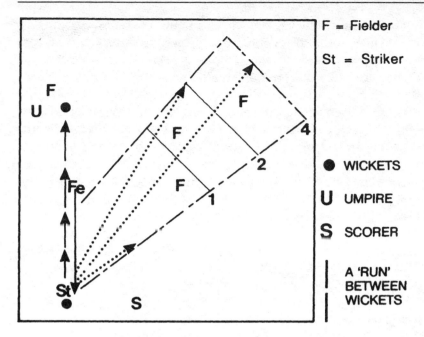

F = Fielder

St = Striker

● WICKETS

U UMPIRE

S SCORER

| A 'RUN'
BETWEEN
WICKETS

Figure 4.9   Game providing central role for fielders

'run out'. (The batter is not out unless a predetermined number of deliveries have been received or a certain number of runs have been scored.)

From the outset, a game-centred approach requires that officials will be needed (part of the games education), thus in this game the 'umpire' judges the run-out as laid down in the laws of cricket and the scorer plays a vital part.

It will not have gone unnoticed that decision-making plays a much greater part in this game, more options are available to the striker: 'Shall I attack the ball and try for a four?'; 'Should I place the ball short and go for a run?', 'Should I risk the run?', 'Perhaps I should play safe?' Well, it all depends... what is the score? How many are needed to win? How many deliveries are left? Where are the fielders placed? The fielders will need to be alert to the different possibilities.

When it is apparent that an intelligent game is being played in the sense that the players know what they should be trying to do, and are trying to do it, further progress can be made. The addition of another batter at the umpire's wicket makes the completion of a run much more difficult – running between the wickets is brought into sharp focus. Another fielder, later to function as a wicket-keeper, is situated to threaten the non-striker. Another umpire is needed.

It is now, and only now, that we make the move from a cooperative feeder to a competitive one. Still using a throw, increase the distance between the batter and bowler and insist on an accurate throw by marking a target area for the bowler. This will have the effect of slowing down the delivery. Operate a system of rewards for hitting the target and a system of penalties for missing it – this will further restrain the competitive bowler and will introduce a 'game' within the game, which now looks like that shown in Figure 4.10.

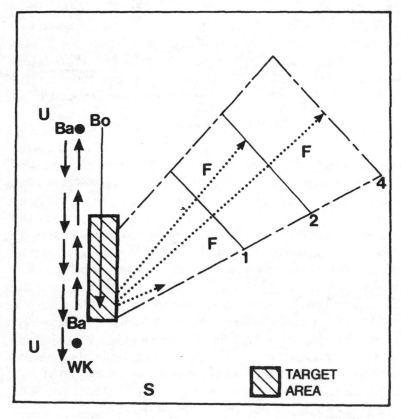

Ba = Batter   Wk = Wicket Keeper   F = Fielder
Bo = Bowler   U = Umpire   S = Scorer

Figure 4.10 Effect on the game of controlled 'bowling'

The task is now much more challenging for the batters as they will have to contend with some deliveries on a 'good length'. But what do we mean by a 'good length'? While it is difficult to say what it is, most would agree that the ball that pitches in the target area, a little short of the batter's reach, is on a 'good length'. Attaking a good length ball is very risky: playing with a 'straight' bat will more often than not spoon the ball into the air, while any contact at all is unlikely when playing with a 'cross' bat as there is such a small striking surface to cover the bounce of the ball. But the option to play defensively by placing the ball into a space and calling for a run is still available. However, if the bowler is pitching consistently on a good length, the fielders will be able to move in to threaten the run. A very tactical game of 5 v 5 cricket is now under way.

Until now the ball has been delivered by means of a throw; now might be the time to introduce youngsters to the 'bowl'. While they should 'have a go' at developing a basic bowling action few of them will be able to establish sufficient control to bowl with the accuracy needed to challenge the batter and to keep the fielders meaningfully involved. For this reason we should be wary of placing too much importance on being able to bowl. In any case, if the rules of Australian indoor cricket, a game rapidly growing in popularity in this country, allow the bowler to deliver the ball underarm from halfway between the wickets, then why can't we do the same in the PE lesson?

Perhaps teachers should take a good look at the various forms of indoor cricket being played (in fact the rules relating to scoring runs in the small side games just described are part and parcel of these games). They do contain some interesting ways in which the game can be shaped in future physical education lessons. It is envisaged in later courses that games will be played in which the batter, increasing the range of shots, is allowed to hit the ball all around the wicket; the fielders, in weighing up the costs and benefits of deploying attacking and defending fields, continue to react to the changing circumstances of the game, and the bowler, in trying to dismiss the batter, is introduced to the notion of 'bowling to the field' – but not with a hard cricket ball.

RUGBY

Accepting that teachers who favour a foundation course will have introduced a free-running, free-passing game like 'lineball' and that many

71

teachers starting rugby play similar sorts of lead-up games, it is worth tracing how basic principles are revisited throughout a games programme.

The basic principle of penetration balanced against risk of loss of possession can be looked at through the eyes of the ball carrier. The basic decision is that of when to run with the ball and when to pass. The focus is perhaps best illustrated by returning to the basics.

Early games

1. 2 *v* 1 keepball stresses the ways of keeping possession by running, dodging, drawing the man and only then passing.
2. 2 *v* 1 speed pass (how many passes in a minute) stresses the assessment of the risks of passing to score and losing possession.

The roles of each player are investigated.

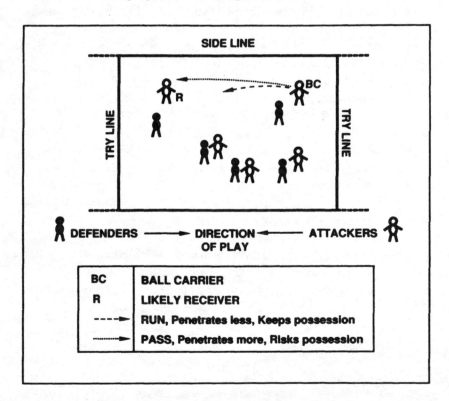

Figure 4.11 Run/pass in lineball

Developing games

Clearly these roles and the risks can be developed through 2 *v* 2 and 4 *v* 4 games that at first are non-directional and then move towards attacking a goal or line.

Lineball – this game has been described earlier and the basic principle is easily seen – to throw the ball forward to a player well down the field penetrates but takes time and because the ball leaves the hands possession might be lost. A run might only make a short penetration but there is no risk of losing possession (Figure 4.11). Is this so different from the fly half's 'kick or pass' decision in rugby or the quarter back's close pass to a running back or long pass to a wide receiver? Of course there is so much more to be learnt in lineball but let us merely take the ball carrier's decision into rugby.

Rugby football is an excellent game for highlighting the relative risks and benefits in running with the ball and keeping possession or kicking with resultant ground gained but possession risked. It is these decisions that make rugby exciting and interesting but of course the game must be simplified if this is to be investigated. After many years of teaching and coaching and, perhaps, more importantly, trying to help others teach rugby, one of us (Rod Thorpe) is convinced that the first game to play following the inclusion of the pass back rule is something like 4 *v* 1 (see Figure 4.12).

The rules of the game are as follows:

1. Attackers have one minute to score as many tries as possible.
2. Once a try is scored run back and start again.
3. If touched stop and pass. (Having a 'flag' [bib] tucked into the waist of the shorts that must be removed to be counted as a touch, ensures no cheating and gives more chance to the runners.)
4. Offences like a dropped ball, interception, or ball thrown forward merely cause the team to return to the start line to begin again.
5. Defender starts on the half-way line until the first pass or run.

The decision to run or pass?

If the ball carrier stands still and passes, what happens? The defender moves across and forward – the attackers have gone nowhere. If the ball carrier runs powerfully and takes on the defender, what might happen? The attacker might beat the defender – the defender has to commit to

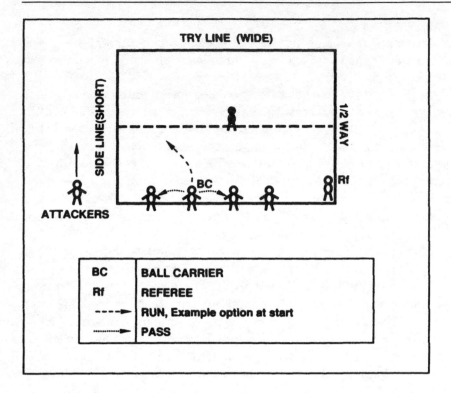

Figure 4.12 4 *v* 1 game including pass back

stop the attacker, therefore other attackers are in space. The ball is in front of supporting players.

It is quite easy to make this into a little competition on a rotation basis. The defender works hard for one minute and carries the tries against him or her as the score. After one minute the defender becomes the referee (for a rest), the referee joins the attacking side, and one attacker becomes the defender. We feel that many children do not enjoy officiating because they only start when the game is complex; why not start when there are only one or two rules? In such a situation stress the following:

- the referee's decision is final;
- no arguing – you are wasting time; and
- defence is important in games.

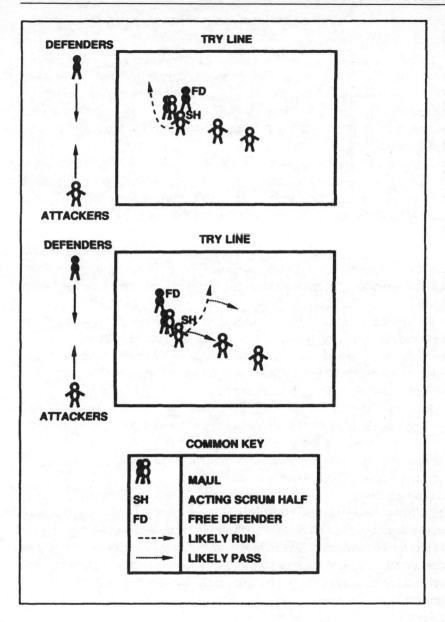

Figure 4.13   Effect of changing position of defenders on running or passing

The game encourages running skills, pace, swerve and scoring tries, passing develops in context.

By moving a few lessons forward the game may be 4 v 2 with a simple touch, hold, maul contact, ie now when the player is touched, she or he must stop, turn and keep the ball available but they can push back toward the try line. The touching defender can embrace the attacker and resist the attacker's push back. A simple controlled contact and maul is present.

The starting positions are exactly as in the first game but now there are two defenders. This can be a competition between three pairs. Each pair defending for two minutes against the other two pairs. (This is quite effective with three pairs of bibs, eg, reds and blues take on yellows.)

The idea of an attacker running to make a defender commit him or herself to stopping the run (by touch or later a tackle) is obvious if you ask the question, 'Do you think it is better to have four against two or three against one?' The answers vary.

Figure 4.13 indicates how committing one defender to the maul and then reacting to the position of the other broadens the decision of whether to run or pass. Of course sometimes we have to go through two mauls to score but often the first defender committed to the maul is left behind and their defence has no depth.

As these elements are practised the sides can become more even but by then the children are becoming aware of the decisions to be made: to run or pass, to commit a player or open up the play, to go to the blind (closed) or open side. Concepts like depth in defence, pressuring the ball, making and using space are all here.

Extracts from videos of adult games can be shown. Forward drives on the blind side that set up runs for the three quarters will illustrate the points developed in the children's simpler game.

The decision about when to move on in the game is based largely on whether the children have grasped the concepts. They may never perfect the skills; that's why top players still play 4 v 2.

A SPORTS EDUCATION

Once children understand the game in the sense that they appreciate the implications of the rules, have investigated the tactics involved, learnt to make appropriate decisions and answered problems as skilfully as they can, is their game development complete? We think not.

Let us suppose that the children have been taught the principles of divided court games, perhaps using throw catch games in year 7 and then moved on to a form of badminton singles and doubles in years 8 and 9. Of course there is a need to practise and consider the finer tactical points but we would see also a need to broaden the knowledge investigated. Perhaps in years 10 and 11 some of the focus should be on badminton in a fuller sense. As youngsters may now be using full courts for singles and doubles there will probably be times when some are sitting out. This seems the ideal time to begin some form of analysis. Our first attempt at this would be to suggest an analysis of the following points:

- How long (time) do the rallies last, how long is the rest between rallies (stop watch and record sheet)? How many times do the players get the shuttlecock back in a five-minute spell (frequency table)?
- How many jumps in the air or sudden spurts (frequency table)?

This information can be followed by basic analysis, discussion and design of on-court drills and off-court training, thus the activity of a lesson might have a different balance, ie matchplay with analyses followed by high intensity exercise – perhaps light, fast, agile. A simple tabulation of the nationalities with players in the 'top 100' can lead to a discussion about the contributing effects of physique, culture or education. Equally, this broadening can fit well with the community link in that the teacher helps children find out where they can play recreationally, play for a team, enter a competition or receive more coaching. This need not take away undue activity time and might well be coordinated within a GCSE course.

We would expect some teachers to be using teaching styles in which children take some responsibility for their own and each other's learning, particularly as we feel sure that most skill practice will be at an individual level. With this background some simple observation of the biomechanics of a movement might be investigated, eg, 'why' and 'how' the racket moves so fast. We have noted some interesting approaches to try and incorporate this form of input with an appropriate assessment for all children.

If a little time is spent in this area at the expense of hitting, but motivation is greatly enhanced to the extent that more children feel inclined to play outside the lesson and see sport as interesting, then this development is well worth while. What we must guard against most carefully with all the children, but particularly with the non-GCSE students, is that this becomes no more than an interesting academic exercise for the teacher.

THE CURRICULUM IN THE SECONDARY SCHOOL

It should now be apparent that if children are to understand the games they play and be fully involved in them both physically and mentally, then we must drastically rethink the way we teach games. Realistically we accept that it may take time to develop a 5–16 games education, but we feel that we have reached a point in our thinking about games that would allow us to propose a secondary games programme that maintains the width necessary to reflect the different focus of games but gives sufficient depth to allow a game to be developed. It should be apparent that the length of time allocated to chosen games may differ. We believe that a person can be given a basic understanding of the game of badminton singles within eight to ten hours but might require perhaps 30 hours to reach a similar position in rugby football.

The programme is based upon the assumption that a specific game is developed along the following lines:

1. It grows out of the appropriate game in the foundation course – using and reinforcing the underlying principles inherent in that type of game.
2. The more specific concepts determined by the particular rules of the specific game are investigated, with parallels made to related games.
3. The game is investigated in the wider context of physical and psychological demands and its place in the community/society. In taking this into account, a secondary programme might look as shown in Table 4.1.

Table 4.1 A games curriculum: time allocation, one hour per week.

Year	Autumn (14 hours)	Spring (14 hours)		Summer (10 hours)
7.	F O U N D A T I O N C O U R S E			
8.	Invasion[a] eg basketball[b]	Court[a] eg badminton[b]	Game[c] X	Fielding[a] eg cricket[b]
9.	Invasion	Court[d]	Game X_1	Fielding
10.	Invasion[e]	Court[e]	Game X_2	Fielding[e]
11.	New game eg lacrosse	Community linked courses		Examination term

(a) Any number of factors will have to be considered when sampling from invasion, court and fielding games.

(b) The sampled games will be continued in years 9 and 10.

(c) A decision might be taken to teach the same game in each of the three years, or the game might change from year to year.

(d) Court games do not require the same allocation of time as they are less complex tactically than the others.

(e) Courses in year 10 are based upon sport education.

CONCLUSION

As we all know, this is a time when fundamental changes have been made in the school curriculum. However, we remain convinced that skill cannot be delivered given the present allocation of time let alone half of it, and that a major revision of our aims and objectives for games teaching is long overdue. Seen in this light, the current trend towards 'benchmarks' and 'behavioural objectives' could be a retrograde step, if we are not careful this will lead down the rocky road to 'tests and measurements' with teachers doing little more than taking a clipboard to the PE lesson.

This cannot be the way ahead. We do not view the games curriculum as a series of piecemeal experiences that somehow come together. The physical education teacher, in selecting a sample of games, must highlight the relationships between them and must develop them working with rule structures, increasing tactical complexity and greater decision-making capacity. It is the ability to think and operate in this way that separates the PE teacher from other providers of games experiences, eg coaches and sports leaders. Teachers should welcome the support of others, particularly with extra-curricular work, but a coherent 'Games Education' leading to a 'Sport Education', must be a major part of the *raison d'etre* of the PE teacher.

REFERENCES

Bunker, D J and Thorpe, R D (1982) 'A model for the teaching of games in secondary school', *Bulletin of Physical Education* **18**(1), pp.5–8.

Thorpe, R D, Bunker, D J and Almond, L (1986) *'Sport Pedagogy'. Proceedings of the OlympicScientific Congress*, Champaign, Ill: Human Kinetics.

CHAPTER FIVE

Reconstructing a new perspective for athletics

Len Almond

INTRODUCTION

In this chapter I will propose a framework for establishing athletics within the physical education programme, especially in primary schools and the middle years of schooling, that could have a significant impact in the later secondary years. In order to stimulate debate and challenge existing thinking about the role of athletics in schools, I shall construct a theoretical position about athletics that has been used as a guideline to try out ideas in primary schools, secondary schools, and with students in higher education. The position that I shall take has been disciplined by practice in schools, which has informed the nature of the framework.

CONSTRUCTING A FRAMEWORK TO DEVELOP ATHLETICS

The framework is based on the idea that from the fundamental movement patterns of children, the raw material of track and field athletics can be identified. Walking, running, throwing and jumping have always been recognized as basic movement patterns (Gallahue, 1982) that provide us with our basic raw material. From these movement patterns it is possible to identify specific challenges that have stood the test of time and have resulted in their selection as competitive events for festivals like the Olympic Games or the World Championships, and the numerous national and local competitions that have been formalized into competitive structures. These competitive structures have been taken as models for athletics in schools; they have influenced the physical education curriculum and the nature of what has been taught, and to some extent restricted their development.

However, it is possible to start with the basic raw material and construct an alternative framework for experiencing athletics in schools. Instead of moving from the raw material of athletics into formal events, I propose that teachers examine their action possibilities, which opens up a whole host of new and different challenges. I am sure that it may

Table 5.1 A classification of action possibilities for athletics

Walking	Acceleration over a short distance
	Endurance activities where pacing is important
Running	Acceleration over a short distance
	Endurance activities where pacing is important
	• with obstacles/barriers (high or long):
	– constant or irregular distance between barriers
	– constant or irregular height of barrier
	• on different terrain and surfaces
	– flat
	– hills
	– uneven surfaces (field/woodland)
	• with partners or individual
Jumping	Hopping, leaping and springing
	• – high
	– long (single, multiple, combination)
	– assisted (eg, pole) high or long
	• – standing or
	– with a run
Throwing	Pulling, pushing, slinging
	• – height
	– distance
	– at targets
	• – sitting
	– standing
	– running

be possible to conceptualize and reconstruct such action possibilities in a number of different ways, but I would like to propose a simple heuristic to take the initiative and present a potential framework. Table 5.1 represents a classification of action possibilities that outlines a potential range of challenges to broaden the athletic experience of all young people. In this framework I see the action possibilities as the basis for recognizing three distinct phases of the athletic experience.

Phase 1   Integrated play
Phase 2   The athletic form
Phase 3   Athletics as a sport.

These phases provide an opportunity for introducing young people to the whole range of athletic experiences and challenges, leading to the opportunity of competing with others, the appreciation of athletic endeavours and the spectacle of an athletic event. As a result there is the possibility that athletics could become an activity that one chooses to pursue because of its inherent satisfactions and it could become an important part of one's life.

THE INTEGRATED PLAY ELEMENT

In the first phase of the framework I believe it is important that young children in the early primary years should be exposed to athletic challenges emerging from the basic raw material of movement. The action possibilities of walking, running, jumping and throwing can be used as a basis for integrating the play element within children's movement education. Thus, running and throwing are part of games experiences, and jumping can be seen as a component of dance and expressive movement and also in gymnastic movement themes. It is possible to construct a whole range of athletic challenges within the integration of play and movement experiences. The major difficulty is to ensure that in the planning process it is possible to achieve coherence as one integrates the action possibilities of athletics with the requirements of games, expressive movement, or gymnastic-type activities. At the same time the skilful teacher has to consider how the whole movement experience can emphasize the joy of being active and the arousal of positive feelings associated with such participation.

83

THE ATHLETIC FORM

Emerging from the integrated play element is a more definite focus, which I call the athletic form. In Figure 5.1 the athletic form has three clear dimensions.

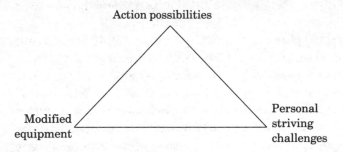

Figure 5.1   The athletic form

The first dimension, the action possibilities, provides guidelines for making a selection of challenges and sampling the potential of athletics. These challenges provide opportunities for testing oneself and striving to improve on one's best. Thus, in the second dimension, personal striving is concerned with attempting to achieve personal targets with an emphasis on the satisfaction to be gained from doing one's best. This is an important point because athletics is often seen as a competition with others in which striving to win is the challenge. In this chapter I would like to make a clear distinction between personal striving and striving to win; the former is a central feature of Phase 2 whereas the later is central to Phase 3.

In athletics young people are usually asked to run against others over a set distance, eg, 80 metres, and at the end a rank order of competitors is produced as a result of the participants striving to outrun their opponents. There is nothing wrong with this so long as it is acknowledged as only one way of indicating success and it is recognized that for some young people such a situation is a negative experience. Those who are obese, or frail, or those who are a long way behind their more mature peers, or whose body clock runs more slowly will repeatedly recognize that they are no good at this activity if they continually come last in a race and a long way behind their peers. There is little likelihood that they will derive satisfaction from this experience. Every time they are

84

asked to compare themselves against others this message is reinforced and they learn that athletics is not for them. Some people would argue that they will find a niche in some other more appropriate activity, but this ignores an important point. If we accept this, we deny young people the opportunity for further development and reinforce the view that rewards are not for effort and determination, but for maturity. As teachers we need to help young people to identify physical education as a good experience and one in which they can try to do their best.

I would argue, therefore, that there is a need to shift the current focus within athletics and recognize that there is a prior concern to an emphasis on striving to win. Personal striving is important as a first priority because it has a different focus in which pupils have the opportunity to achieve satisfaction from their performance and to monitor their achievements. The challenges in Phase 2 provide opportunities for all pupils to experience success from their efforts and recognize improvements in performance. One example will serve to illustrate this. A class can be divided into pairs, one running and one assisting with recording achievement, and set the challenge of seeing how far they can run in four seconds. Their achievement is recorded by their partner. Each pupil will usually exceed their first efforts or at least be very close. The shift in focus ensures that pupils are striving against their own efforts and social comparison is not used to indicate success. Some critics may retort that young people will automatically compare what they have done with others. Of course, some pupils will do this, but time after time when I have demonstrated this, observers have noted that pupilsare centrally concerned with their own performance and satisfaction comes from their own efforts.

In the third dimension it is necessary to modify equipment, especially for hurdling and throwing challenges, in order that the technical limitations imposed by inappropriate equipment, eg, heavy shots and a large discus, are reduced. Thus, in hurdling the type of barriers, the height, and the distances between each barrier can be modified. Too often young people have to adjust to the inappropriate demands of the event rather than modify the event to enable a person to perform adequately. Hurdling is about the rhythm of moving fast over a specified distance with obstacles that have set distances between them. Thus, if we start off with the idea of three strides and striding over an obstacle, we can teach young people the rhythm of hurdling, and increase the distance between obstacles and their height as they become more competent and acquire the confidence to run fast over a barrier. In throwing, a whole range of new objects can be introduced, eg, quoits or hoops for slinging actions; netballs/footballs/volleyballs for heaving, pushing and slinging; old worn-out rounders bats or rhythmic gymnastic clubs for pulling actions; old woollen socks filled with sand or blasting shot for pushing, pulling, or slinging. The important point is not to be restricted by current conceptions of what constitute adult throwing implements.

During this phase it is unnecessary to emphasize the technical aspects of performance, but it is important to ensure that challenges are underpinned by the use of key teaching cues or principles of action, eg in throwing think of 'long and tall'. At this stage key words become part of a pupil's vocabulary that they can incorporate into their performances. The challenges that teachers present need to be underpinned by key biomechanical principles in order that key root movements can become part of the pupil's experiences of athletics. Therefore the kind of challenge that is presented, the key words used to reinforce it, and teacher interventions provide the means for developing major root movements.

ATHLETICS AS A SPORT

The dominant focus in Phase 2 was the idea that athletic challenges should have a personal context in which all pupils can recognize that athletics can be personally rewarding and that achievement can be a product of their own efforts. From this phase of the athletic form, the third phase emerges as 'athletics as a sport'. After Phase 2 many young people will wish to test themselves against others in structural competitive situations. In such a context teachers and coaches will wish to provide opportunities to compete appropriate to pupils' developing physical needs, and mindful of long-term developments. Thus, young people can learn how to compete, how to enjoy the struggle of a 'good' competition, and recognize that thorough preparation is part of producing one's best and stretching one's capabilities. In addition they can learn to respect other competitors and see them not as obstacles to their own success but as contributors to a 'good' contest.

Phase 3, which can be seen in Figure 5.2, contains three major components:

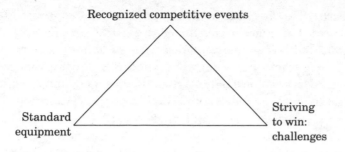

Figure 5.2   Athletics as a sport

1. Recognized competitive events
2. Standard equipment
3. Striving to win: challenges.

The action possibilities of Phase 2 become more formalized so that competition can take place within a clearly defined range of events. The equipment required for these events may have to be modified in order to reduce any technical limitations, but there is a clear emphasis on standard distances, implements and regulations governing conduct so that a structure for competition against others can take place. As a sport the challenges within Phase 3 are based on striving to win where one attempts to excel worthy opponents. Here the challenge is clearly one in which rank orders are established and participants are aware of this point and still wish to compete.

During Phase 3 athletes will wish to practise in order to enhance their performances. Thus, at this stage the idea of a basic working model, arising from the root movement patterns of Phase 2, is introduced to enable performers to execute movement patterns effectively and with maximum efficiency. But such a working model needs to be seen as a whole movement and not a scaled-down version of adult performers. A basic working model is a representation of mature movement and not simply a mini-version. This idea is important for young people because there is a danger that the technical requirements of an event will be broken down and specific features rehearsed over and over again. Also, there is the danger that some techniques adopted by young athletes, even though they appear effective, are dead-end models that lead the athlete down a path that may be impossible to change and may impair future improvements. There is a need to provide basic working models that incorporate the technical demands of an event, appropriate biomechanical principles and the rhythm of an event in action.

If teachers and coaches can be provided with guidance about basic root movements and a working model which retains the very essence of performing a whole movement, I believe these will be more appropriate than many of the lead-up movements that teachers are using at present. This is not new. Dick (1986) has made proposals for a technical model and this has taken us some way along my route, but these technical models need to be translated into practical exemplars, just for teachers, with the realities of schools in mind, and made accessible on a wide scale in the form of curriculum guidelines for athletics. Much of the current literature in athletics has excellent technical points but it rarely tackles the problem of how young people can grasp athletics in its simplest form within a school physical education programme.

ALTERNATIVE USES FOR ATHLETICS

We must not assume that the only potential use of school athletics is the preparation for competitive situations. Some young people, after their involvement in Phase 2, may not choose to enter into competitions against others and yet they may wish to continue with athletics. We should respect this right and consider what provision we could make to maintain their interest and commitment.

Some young people will continue to enjoy being challenged in an athletic context; others may choose running for their health or simply enjoy the satisfaction of being active. It may be that athletic challenges in unusual forms could be part of a festival of activity in which teams compete for recognition or acclaim within the school or between schools. The television programme 'It's a Knockout' provided the inspiration for constructing a festival that stimulates and awakens interest in athletic challenges that are more open-ended and exhilarating. Such a festival would require preparation in the form of conditioning, planning and identifying appropriate challenges that simulate what they might expect on the day.

In the same way, school sports days and athletics meetings could be injected with more imagination and originality to enable large groups to participate, using a range of alternative athletic challenges – including competition against others – so that the whole school could obtain real value from the occasion. Instead of repeating the same type of sports day each year, examine alternatives that involve the whole school, or a year group, and generate excitement, commitment and the satisfactions of enjoying athletics. If your sports day does this, fine, but check this out by undertaking an inquiry into what pupils, staff and parents actually feel about the day and preparation for the day.

CONCLUSION

In conclusion, I would like to summarize what I am proposing. First, I am suggesting that athletics should be based on the action possibilities that arise from the raw material of athletic movement. These action possibilities provide a framework for reconstructing athletics in order to explore their potential as athletic challenges in a physical education programme. Such a reconstruction should involve three phases that provide a lead into athletics as a competitive sporting activity and provide the means by which young people can either choose to opt into a competitive situation against others or continue with athletics as an opportunity for personal striving. Underpinning an individual's performance is the need to learn root movements and a basic working model to enhance their achievement.

REFERENCES

Dick, F (1986) *But First...*, London: British Amateur Athletic Board.
Gallahue, D L (1982) *Understanding Motor Development in Children*, New York: John Wiley.

CHAPTER SIX

Gymnastics in the physical education curriculum

Lorraine Cale

INTRODUCTION

Given the long tradition gymnastics has in the PE curriculum, it was perhaps no surprise that when the National Curriculum for physical education (NCPE) was introduced in September 1990, it was identified as one of the six activity areas. Gymnastics or gymnastic activities are a component of the NCPE for all age groups. Indeed, only three activities, namely games, dance and gymnastics are given this status in the revised curriculum (Department for Education [DFE] and Welsh Office [WO], 1995). Gymnastics is compulsory throughout the primary school, being one of three activity areas that must be taught at KS1 and one of six at KS2, and becomes optional at secondary school. At KS3, pupils must do either gymnastics or dance but teachers can choose to deliver the whole programme of study (units A and B) or just one half unit (unit A). However, despite its long tradition and the prominent position gymnastics has been afforded in the NCPE, developments in gymnastics have not always been smooth. Concern has been expressed that school gymnastics has witnessed a decline over the past 20 years (Smith, 1989a). In 1985/86 an HMI survey revealed a poor and depressing picture of the state of gymnastics in schools and Smith (1989a) reports how a decline has been seen in both the amount and quality of gymnastics taught. Indeed, Smith (1989b) warned that if positive steps were not taken to improve and revitalize gymnastics in schools its future was very bleak.

The decline in school gymnastics has partly been blamed on the confusion that arose in the 1950s and 1960s from the dichotomy between the traditional skills-based approach to teaching gymnastics and the Laban-inspired modern educational approach. Modern educational gymnastics placed the individual child at the centre of the philosophy and aimed to extend a child's tendency for natural movement while fostering expression of individuality. Smith (1989b) claimed, however, that the philosophy of modern educational gymnastics and its accompanying material were difficult for some teachers to grasp. A divide thus developed between advocates of the educational gymnastics approach and the more traditional skills or artistic gymnastics approach. The two approaches, 'educational' and 'artistic', became viewed as bi-polar opposites. This division confused and even hindered many teachers, lecturers and students and certainly did little to help develop confidence in the area. Teachers were uncertain about what to teach and how to teach it.

Fortunately, in the 1980s a reappraisal of gymnastics was undertaken by specialist PE lecturers, advisers, inspectors, coaches and some teachers (Wright, 1991). Wright (1991) identifies a number of events as being of particular importance in the reappraisal process. These included the deliberations of the British Association of Advisers and Lecturers in Physical Education (BAALPE) Working Party on Gymnastics between 1985 and 1988 and the attendant publications; the deliberations of specialist lecturers, advisers and teachers; the presentation of simplified theoretical frameworks for teaching gymnastics; the refinement of micro teaching video techniques and other publications.

Such developments, while perhaps being long overdue, were welcomed by the profession and marked the beginnings of real progress. They helped to clarify and stabilize teaching methods and lessen so much of the confusion that had arisen in the past. Following the reappraisal a degree of consensus emerged towards 'methodological and philosophical integration' or, as Smith (1989b) puts it, 'the marriage of two ideologies living under one gymnastics roof' (p.75). Quite simply, it was realized that the bi-polar approaches were capable of being integrated. According to Smith (1989b) the scope of the integration lies along a continuum that is broad enough to accommodate variations of style

91

and approach but narrow enough to enable conceptual practicability. In this respect teachers can find their preferences of style and approach somewhere along the continuum. Thus current ideas on the teaching of gymnastics have developed from the integration of past teaching methods. With this background in mind we need now to turn to gymnastics in the 1990s. This chapter considers the nature, scope and value of gymnastics as a curriculum activity in the 1990s. In addition, some of the major issues in teaching gymnastics and some of the more pressing concerns for the future development of the activity are identified.

THE CONTRIBUTION OF GYMNASTIC ACTIVITIES TO THE CURRICULUM

It is interesting that the NCPE refers to 'gymnastic activities'. In adopting this term it seems that gymnastics is being referred to in an holistic sense with the implication that it should be broad based and perhaps include all gymnastic forms. Gymnastics encompasses much more than artistic or educational gymnastics; it also includes sports acrobatics, rhythmic gymnastics, remedial gymnastics, display gymnastics and trampolining. Indeed, the National Curriculum proposals for physical education (DES and WO, 1991) acknowledge that at KS4 gymnastic activities include the above, plus body conditioning and health-based fitness work, diving, martial arts and even synchronized swimming. Thus, gymnastics should not be taken to mean merely floorwork or large apparatus work as so often still seems to be the case in many schools. This represents a very narrow and restrictive definition and immediately limits both the activities movement and enjoyment potential.

All gymnastic activities focus on the body and the actions of the body are central in the skilful execution of movement skills. Successful execution of gymnastic elements demands physical development and the development of skill. The rationale for the inclusion of gymnastics as an activity area in the NCPE was that:

> gymnastic activities focus on the body. They are concerned with acquiring control, co-ordination and versatility in the use of the body in increasingly challenging situations and with developing strength, especially of the upper body, and maintaining flexibility. (DES and WO, 1991, p.76)

Smith (1991) summarizes the contribution gymnastics can make to a child's development by drawing attention to three areas: physical development, body management and fostering individuality. In terms of physical development, gymnastics is an excellent activity for improving muscular strength and endurance, flexibility and aerobic endurance. It is furthermore highly desirable as a conditioning activity in that it is weight-bearing, involving both the lower and upper extremities. In this respect, and as highlighted later in this chapter, it can contribute most effectively to health-related work. Body management refers to the acquisition of knowledge of how the body moves and responds to external forces, while the notion of individuality refers to the way in which gymnastics enables children to work creatively and inventively. Gymnastics' unique ability to foster individuality makes it a particularly valuable activity area within the PE curriculum.

By comparison, other activity areas (with the exception of dance) offer limited opportunities for creativity. Gymnastics, however, offers an ideal opportunity for children to explore, develop and create their own movement ideas. During lessons children should be involved in their own learning and should be afforded the opportunity to develop something that is theirs and that is original. Creating even a short phrase of movement demands creativity and calls on the children's individual expression.

According to Wright (1992), to allow individuality to flower other aspects of child development also need to take place. These include the development of confidence, curiosity, an increasingly broad repetoire of skills, a willingness to play creatively (explore) with any movement pattern, a capacity for thinking fluently and originally, a capacity for problem-solving, a capacity to exercise independent judgement and select and refine material, and finally an expanding conception of the range of movement possibilities that each area of material being studied makes possible.

Another unique feature of gymnastics is that it is an aesthetic activity. The gymnastic environment offers an effective context for developing aesthetic appreciation. Aesthetic appreciation and experience are concerned with heightened awareness of movement qualities such as line, form, design and dynamics. The range of qualities that can be expressed in gymnastics is extensive and these should be incorporated into lessons from the outset.

The aesthetic nature of the activity is highlighted in the programmes of study for gymnastics. At KS2 children are required to emphasize changes of shape, speed and direction through gymnastic actions, and at KS3 children should be taught to move fluently, to include variety, contrast and repetition in their work and to address the factors that influence quality in performance including extension, body tension and clarity of body shape. Clearly these requirements refer to the aesthetic dimension of the activity and are included in the curriculum to develop children's aesthetic appreciation and experience.

DELIVERING GYMNASTICS IN THE CURRICULUM

Despite the degree of consensus that was reached in the teaching of gymnastics in the late 1980s, many teachers still often seem confused about both the approach and the teaching styles they should adopt in their gymnastic programmes. Gymnastics teaching should not be straitjacketed into one particular approach and one particular teaching style. If the approaches lie along a continuum, teachers should feel free to move to the left and right of this continuum quite freely, as and when they wish.

Teachers may wish to vary their approach and teaching styles depending on the content to be covered. For example, there are times when it might be very appropriate for a particular skill to be taught by means of the traditional skills-based approach and this might be delivered in a very direct way (command style). Providing children are working within their skill threshold this may be very effective. Other content, however, might lend itself more to the educational approach and may draw on a range of teaching styles (such as inclusion and guided discovery).

Of course, some teachers may always prefer to work at approximately the same point along the artistic–educational continuum and may alter their approach very little. There is certainly no problem with this but if this is the case teachers should still be encouraged to incorporate a variety of teaching styles into their lessons, reflecting the diversity of the material to be covered in gymnastics as well as the diversity of children's needs. Indeed, the language of the NCPE (which includes the terms *plan*, *perform*, *explore*, *develop*, *devise*, *select*, *practise*, *repeat*, *refine*, *adapt*, *improve*, *understand*, *assess* and *evaluate* in the end of Key Stage Descriptions and Programmes of Study for gymnastics) encourages and implies the need for the adoption of a range of teaching styles to meet such requirements.

The vocabulary also highlights the need for children to be involved in the learning process and increasingly to become independent learners. Thus as children progress, their gymnastics teachers should adapt their styles accordingly so that children become less dependent on them for ideas. As Jo Harris points out in Chapter 7, the National Curriculum is about content, not delivery and it allows scope for professional judgement regarding how best to transmit content within the context of particular schools. There is then, certainly no right or wrong way to deliver gymnastics and teachers should have the confidence to decide the approach and styles of teaching they feel most comfortable with.

While flexibility and choice in teaching methods are strongly advocated and encouraged, gymnastic lessons do, however, still need a focus or particular emphasis. For children, a lesson with a focus will enable them to contextualize their learning and understand the direction their gymnastics experience is taking. For teachers, a focus facilitates planning. Rigid adherence to a theme for a series of lessons has been criticized in the past on the grounds that it leads to a 'narrowness' of movement experience and boredom for pupils. However, with good planning teachers should be able to develop lessons that are varied and challenging and that can sustain the interest of pupils.

Regardless of the approach and teaching styles adopted, certain principles should always be adhered to in teaching gymnastics. Jo Harris, in Chapter 7, refers to 'caring teaching strategies'. Such strategies should be incorporated in all lessons to ensure that children are afforded positive, challenging, meaningful and as far as possible enjoyable gymnastic experiences. Gymnastics can be a fearful activity and it is imperative that children feel safe and not threatened in the gymnastic environment. Differentiation in gymnastics is vital to ensure that children are able to work within their own range of ability and achieve success in the tasks they are set. Teachers need to provide choices in tasks to make the content accessible to all pupils. If tasks are set that offer no scope for a varied response, then care must be taken to ensure that the tasks are still accessible to all. A situation should never arise where children are excluded from an activity on the basis of their ability.

Furthermore, gymnastics should be challenging. Movement responses should be possible to all tasks, but the tasks must still be demanding and bring a sense of achievement when answered. Children should also be encouraged to practise and refine their movement responses at all times. While experimenting and exploring with movement material is an important part of the learning process in gymnastics and vital in terms of fostering individuality, time must be allocated within lessons for the refinement of material. Innovation and experimentation should be encouraged but not at the expense of quality; rather, the two should be developed and encouraged hand-in-hand. I agree entirely with the comments made by Bob Smith when he recommends that 'we must produce a system which requires that children think for themselves and respond rationally to movement situations and problems... and experience high quality movement' (Smith, 1989b, p.79).

As well as challenge, gymnastics should offer variety. Both can be achieved within lessons in a number of ways, the most common of which include combining floor and apparatus work, varying the physical demands of the activities, varying group dynamics (exploring with individual, pair and group work), and by allowing children to be involved in their own learning.

In addition, a much under-utilized means of achieving variety is the incorporation of a range of gymnastic activities. As mentioned earlier, gymnastic activities encompass a variety of forms and include more than just floor and large apparatus work. Indeed, Smith (1989b) believes that the practice of teaching only one aspect of gymnastics is narrow, restrictive and counter-productive. The recent growth in the popularity of other gymnastic forms such as sports acrobatics and rhythmic gymnastics has already encouraged many teachers to broaden their curriculum and offer children new and varied gymnastic experiences. Indeed, the National Curriculum proposals for physical education (DES and WO, 1991) suggest that towards the end of KS3, sports acrobatics, rhythmic gymnastics and trampolining may be introduced into the gymnastics programme and the document highlights how at KS4 gymnastics should include artistic and rhythmic gymnastics, sports acrobatics and compositional gymnastics.

Sports acrobatics has certainly provided many teachers with a wealth of new pair and group work ideas. It is a social activity, giving children the opportunity to work with, develop trust in and cooperate with peers. Furthermore, it is an ideal progression from floorwork in that it requires no additional or specialized gymnastic equipment. Similarly, rhythmic gymnastics, which involves the use of hand apparatus such as hoops, ribbons and balls, also affords many additional new skills and composition possibilities. It is an extremely versatile and creative form of gymnastics with a surprisingly low initial skill threshold. Rhythmicgymnastics apparatus is relatively inexpensive, certainly compared to larger pieces of apparatus, and thus the activity may form an attractive and economical alternative within the gymnastics curriculum.

At KS4, as mentioned earlier, the National Curriculum proposals also identify other gymnastic activities to include body conditioning and health-based fitness work, diving, martial arts and synchronized swimming. Some older pupils in particular may be more interested in the fitness/body conditioning aspects of gymnastics and there is certainly scope at KS4 for pupils to develop their own conditioning programmes. The Programme of Study for gymnastics at KS4 involves planning and implementing a training schedule relevant to the gymnastic activities undertaken. In this respect gymnastics takes on a whole new meaning and is perhaps made more meaningful and relevant to older age groups. Smith (1989b) stresses the importance of a gymnastics curriculum that has some relevance in the lives of children and that will give them something that will be useful in post-school life. Clearly this is an important issue if gymnastics is to be an accepted component throughout the PE curriculum.

In teaching gymnastics teachers should also appreciate and take advantage of the contribution the activity can make to the personal and social development of children. Personal and social education (PSE) is a cross-curricular dimension of the National Curriculum and according to National Curriculum Council (NCC) Circular No. 6 is the responsibility of all teachers. PE's contribution and role generally in PSE has been widely recognized and is highlighted in the National Curriculum proposals for PE (DES and WO, 1991). Wright (1992) stresses the need for teachers to exploit the various opportunities gymnastics lessons offer to contribute to PSE. For example, gymnastics may contribute to the personal, social and moral development of children in sympathetic and safe cooperation in handling apparatus, the unselfish sharing of apparatus and space, cooperative activities (partner work or assisting a partner in skill acquisition), the appreciation and acceptance of the different abilities and qualities of peers and in the sensitive sharing and showing of work. Underwood and Williams (1991) highlight the way in which PSE can take place in gymnastics through the adoption of different teaching styles and strategies such as reciprocal teaching or cooperative learning. Within these styles pupils are encouraged to take some responsibility for their and other's learning and to work with and help others. Potential and additional benefits to be gained from such approaches include the development of communication, observational, analytical and social skills.

Finally, the contribution gymnastics can make to other areas of the NCPE should be realized, for example towards meeting the general requirements for physical education and the health-related exercise components of the curriculum. Gymnastics is an ideal activity in which to address elements within the general requirements such as the development of positive attitudes by being mindful of others and the environment; and ensuring safe practice by learning to lift, carry, place and use equipment safely and follow safety procedures.

In terms of health-based work, acknowledgement of the importance of gymnastics in the physical preparation of the body is well established. Physical improvements are achieved in gymnastics by the management and manipulation of one's own body weight. Smith (1991) notes how improving the capacities of muscular strength and endurance, flexibility and cardiovascular endurance are key features when gymnastics is used to make a contribution to the development of a child's health and fitness. Given that gymnastics draws on such components of fitness it is an ideal activity through which to reinforce or, if teachers feel confident, to deliver the knowledge base associated with these health-related exercise components. Indeed, the National Curriculum proposals for PE note how each area of activity within the PE curriculum lends itself to the reinforcement of certain health-related exercise concepts and how gymnastics provides a suitable medium in which to reinforce the knowledge base and experiences associated with flexibility and muscular strength and endurance (DES and WO, 1991). In planning a gymnastics programme Smith (1991) recommends that every lesson should have a physical element to it both from a practical point of view, (ie, the doing) and from a cognitive point of view (ie, thinking about and understanding about the doing).

CONCERNS FOR THE FUTURE DEVELOPMENT OF CURRICULUM GYMNASTICS

It seems that the trend in schools gymnastics over the past decades has been one of chequered development and general decline. Turning to the future though, given its reappraisal in the 1980s and more recently its place in the National Curriculum, is this trend likely to be reversed? Certainly with the problems gymnastics has encountered in the past, the activity needed to be given a prominent position within the NCPE. However, while gymnastics is identified as an activity area at all four Key Stages, the reality is that it is only compulsory at Key Stages 1 and 2.

At secondary level gymnastics becomes an optional activity and can be dropped from the curriculum. This means that potentially many children's gymnastic experience could take place soley in the primary school and be taught by non-specialists. At present many primary school teachers are reaching saturation point with the implementation of all National Curriculum subjects. As a result, physical education, being only a foundation subject, is likely to be low on their list of priorities. Wright (1991), while not wishing to lay blame upon primary teachers in any way, acknowledges that those who are strikingly effective in their gymnastics teaching tend to be the exception. He blames initial teacher education and the lack of time available to prepare teachers in many primary courses, claiming that many teachers leave college ill-equipped to teach PE and hence gymnastics confidently and effectively. Indeed, concern about the inadequacy of initial teacher education in preparing primary teachers to teach PE satisfactorily has been a recurring feature of the Physical Education Association for some time. Clearly, it is a great shame if children are not being taught effectively in the primary schools because this is the time when real gains in movement capabilities can be made. Young children have a natural flexibility and are highly creative in their thinking. They are also usually highly motivated and thirsty for activity and the adventure that a stimulating gymnastics environment can provide.

If children encounter poor and inadequate gymnastics teaching at primary school this undoubtedly has a knock-on effect into the secondary school. Secondary teachers often find that even the very basic work needs to be addressed with year 7 pupils before they can progress to more advanced work. However, it appears that poor gymnastics teaching is not just a primary school problem. Many specialist PE teachers also leave college ill-equipped to teach gymnastics confidently and effectively. Smith (1989a) expresses concern that young teachers appear to lack confidence and be inadequately prepared to teach gymnastics in schools. He blames this situation on the fact that students often arrive at higher education institutions with little or no previous experience of gymnastics and then have to learn how to teach it with limited time and resources. The danger then is that students enter teaching nervous about tackling gymnastics and as a result may adopt an 'avoid at all costs' attitude towards the area.

Improvements in initial teacher education and INSET provision are the most obvious possible solutions to the problems teachers face in delivering curriculum gymnastics. Wright (1992) believes massive in-service training programmes and significant changes in initial teacher education to be essential to equip a modest proportion of teachers. Inservice work needs to be arranged that will give teachers the confidence to tackle gymnastics and enable them to appreciate the scope that the activity offers.

Other pressing concerns for the future development and progress of gymnastics relate to the time allocation for PE, the organization of the PE curriculum and whether teachers have the time to deliver gymnastics effectively. In a survey of physical education in secondary schools, Harris (1994) revealed that curriculum time for PE has steadily declined over the past few decades and most heads of department consider the time allocated for their subject to be inadequate to meet the needs of the National Curriculum.

Similarly, another secondary school survey conducted in one Local Education Authority (LEA) in 1991, revealed that many teachers were crying out for more time for PE. Interestingly, and perhaps more importantly, 27 per cent indicated a need for more time for gymnastics (Penney and Evans, 1994). It has been reported that many primary schools devote one or two half-hour periods a week to gymnastics during the autumn and spring terms each year (Wright, 1991). In this respect, Wright (1991) suggests that available curriculum time in primary schools is less of a constraint. However, in secondary schools, the breadth of PE programmes provided (and I would suggest the dominance of team games within the curriculum) often limits gymnastics to the equivalent of one hour a week for one term in each of the first three years. Indeed, even these figures appear somewhat on the optimistic side.

The reality is that team games still dominate the curriculum of most schools (Penney and Evans, 1994; Sports Council, 1993) thus eating into the time available for other activity areas. Indeed, with the increased emphasis on competitive team games in the revised NCPE (DFE and WO, 1995), this dominance seems likely to persist for the foreseeable future. Clearly, with such limited time, the children's gymnastics experience and what they can be expected to achieve within this experience will undoubtedly be limited.

While gymnastics does not appear to be a popular activity for many teachers for reasons already outlined, it seems that it is similarly not a popular activity for many children and in particular for boys. A national survey of young people and sport conducted by the Sports Council in 1994 revealed that gymnastics failed to rank in the top five sports for boys and girls. Three in ten boys and two in ten girls of secondary age listed it as an activity they did not enjoy. Furthermore, when children were asked what sports they did out of lessons, gymnastics was not amongst the top ten most frequently mentioned for boys or girls. Wright (1991, p.9) asks, 'Can it [gymnastics] come alive for pupils in our schools, whatever their physiques and temperaments?' If it can not, and if we as physical educators can not make it come alive for pupils then we are clearly failing them and denying them the positive experiences they deserve and gymnastics can potentially afford. We need to ask what we can do to promote gymnastics to both teachers and pupils such that it is viewed as a worthwhile activity area and one that is worth pursuing throughout the PE curriculum. Essential in the promotion of the area is good teaching coupled with adherence to the principles highlighted earlier in the chapter. Gymnastics needs to be able to provide positive, challenging, meaningful, relevant, varied and enjoyable experiences for pupils of all ages.

Finally, perhaps the cause of gymnastics over the years has not been helped by the increasing concern over the safety of the activity. I am involved in delivering INSET courses for primary and secondary teachers on gymnastics and during this work I have often been barraged by questions on safety issues. Teachers frequently pose general safety questions with regards to the gymnastic environment: the placing of equipment, the type of equipment that is safe and unsafe to use, as well as more specific questions regarding the safety of executing certain gymnastic elements or skills. Fears that particular elements are in fact now deemed dangerous or contraindicated have concerned a number of teachers and even discouraged some from tackling the activity and certain skills all together.

While it is encouraging that increased attention is now being paid to safety issues within gymnastics (and indeed in all areas of activity) regrettably, there seems to be still a lot of confusion surrounding the whole area. It has come to my attention that a number of quite safe gymnastic elements are being discouraged within certain authorities and schools because they are mistakenly believed to be dangerous. The safety of skills such as backwards rolls and shoulder stands, for example, have been questioned and they have even been banned in some schools with no real rationale. Teachers unsure about the safety of particular elements or practices in gymnastics are encouraged to read the excellent section on 'Safe and unsafe exercises' in a book by Harris and Elbourn (1992).

CONCLUSION

In the last few years teaching methods in gymnastics have been clarified and seem to have stabilized. Such stability, coupled with the statutory place gymnastics has been afforded in the NCPE, provides teachers with a sound foundation and direction for their work in the 1990s. As has been noted, gymnastics has endless possibilities and a range of benefits, both physical and psychological. These need to be fully appreciated and exploited and awareness needs to be raised of the potential of the activity for all children. In addition, careful attention needs to be paid to how gymnastics is approached and delivered such that it provides positive, challenging, meaningful and varied experiences for children.

However, despite the valuable contribution gymnastics makes to the curriculum, there are limitations to what can be achieved. Concerns over poor gymnastics teaching and teacher training, inadequate resources and inadequate time allocation for the activity suggest that there is still some way to go if gymnastics is to fully recover from the decline it has experienced over the years. Teachers need practical help in the form of inservice provision and better initial teacher training in gymnastics, in addition to guaranteed PE curriculum time, resources, and facilities if they are to meet the National Curriculum requirements and develop effective gymnastics programmes.

The next few years will be an interesting time for gymnastics. As the National Curriculum settles down and teachers come to terms with the changes, hopefully it will receive the recognition, attention and time it deserves and will once again make real strides as a valued and important curriculum activity.

REFERENCES

DES and the WO (1991) *Physical Education for ages 5 to 16*, London: HMSO.

DFE and the WO (1995) *Physical Education in the National Curriculum*, London: HMSO.

Harris, J (1994) 'Physical education in the National Curriculum: is there enough time to be effective?', *The British Journal of Physical Education*, **25**(4), 34–8.

Harris, J and Elbourn, J (1992) 'Warming up and cooling down. Practical ideas for implementing the physical education National Curriculum', Loughborough University.

Penney, D and Evans, J (1994) 'It's just not (and not just) cricket', *The British Journal of Physical Education*, **25**(3), 9–12.

Smith, B (1989a) 'Schools gymnastics – guidelines for teaching', *The British Journal of Physical Education*, Autumn, 3, 132–4.

Smith, B (1989b) 'Curriculum developments in gymnastics' in *The Place of Physical Education in Schools*, L Almond (ed.), London: Kogan Page, pp.72–81.

Smith, B (1991) 'The contribution of gymnastics to health based work', *The British Journal of Physical Education*, Winter, 4, 23–5.

Sports Council (1993) *Children's Sports Participation 1991/92*, Cardiff: Sports Council for Wales.

Sports Council (1995) *Young People and Sport in England, 1994*, London: Sports Council.

Underwood, M and Williams, A (1991) 'Personal and social education through gymnastics', *The British Journal of Physical Education*, Winter, 4, 15–19.

Wright, J (1991) 'Gymnastics-ideals for the 1990's', *The British Journal of Physical Education*, Winter, 4, 9–14.

Wright, J (1992) 'Gymnastics in the National Curriculum' in *New Dimensions in Physical Education. Volume 2 Towards a National Curriculum*, N Armstrong (ed.), Champaign, Ill.: Human Kinetics, pp.123–39.

CHAPTER SEVEN

A health focus in physical education

Jo Harris

INTRODUCTION

A look back over the last seven years reveals a number of significant developments in the relationship between physical education and health. Health-related exercise (HRE), the understanding, skills and attitudes associated with the adoption of active lifestyles, is now written into the National Curriculum (NC) for all age groups, both within physical education (PE) and as a component of the cross-curricular theme of health education (HE) (DFE and WO, 1995; DES and WO, 1992; NCC, 1990). A survey carried out one year after the introduction of the National Curriculum for physical education (NCPE) revealed that most secondary schools were delivering HRE in some form or another within the PE curriculum (Harris, 1994a; 1995).

In the same year as the launch of the NCPE, the results of the first ever national fitness survey on the 16-plus age group became known (Sports Council and HEA, 1992) and the government published *The Health of the Nation* White Paper, which acknowledged the role of physical activity in promoting good health and recognized the value of school PE in teaching young people the necessary skills and understanding associated with adopting an active way of life (Department of Health [DoH], 1992). One of the future planned outcomes of the government's focus on health is a major nationwide promotion of physical activity emphasizing the strengths of a coordinated and collaborative approach to encouraging 'more people to be more active more often'. The government White Paper and the more recent physical activity consultation paper (DoH, 1995) are well supported by a publication from the medical profession summarizing the range of health benefits that can be accrued by young and old through regular physical activity (Royal College of Physicians [RCP], 1991) and by ongoing research findings on the health benefits of moderate intensity activity (cited in DoH, 1995). Indeed, within the last few years there has been increasingly widespread promotion of physical activity, especially in primary health care with GPs being encouraged to guide their patients towards an active way of life.

The last seven years have also witnessed an increase in research on children's activity levels (Armstrong and Bray, 1991; Armstrong et al., 1990; Cale and Almond, 1992; Sleap and Warburton, 1992; Sports Council, 1995) and on the development of specific recommendations relating to the amount of exercise that children and adolescents should be doing to improve their health (Corbin, et al., 1994; Sallis and Patrick, 1994). Furthermore, there has been increasing interest from within the fitness industry in Great Britain in the development of training courses for exercise teachers and leaders working with children, the intention being to help them appreciate that children respond differently from adults to exercise and have different needs and desires.

The above developments represent positive moves in the area of children's exercise and health during the 1990s. So is there any disappointing news to report? Unfortunately, yes. First, the results of the research to date present a far from rosy picture of children's and adults' activity levels. The indications are that only about a third to a half of children and adults in England are doing enough exercise to benefit their health (Cale and Almond, 1992; Sports Council and HEA, 1992). It would seem that sedentary lifestyles are commonplace and that, while physical activity is considered to be 'good for you', it is simply not done on a regular basis by most people. However, the difficulties of accurately measuring activity levels is accepted and further research is necessary to confirm the concerns and to establish more precisely the minimal and optimal levels of exercise associated with specific health gains (Riddoch and Boreham, 1995). In the meantime, the PE profession needs to consider its role with respect to increasing children's activity levels and to providing appropriate guidance to children on recommended volumes of exercise.

Second, with respect to physical education's role in promoting health, there appears to be much confusion, ambivalence and rhetoric within the physical education profession. For example, what are physical education teachers supposed to make of apparent dichotomies and anomolies such as: (a) aiming for a balanced PE programme alongside a government 'push' on competitive team games; (b) aiming to educate, involve and motivate every child within the PE curricular and extra-curricular programme yet feeling under pressure to win trophies with a minority of the more talented pupils; (c) combating children's low activity levels with reduced PE time; and (d) delivering HRE in a way that is considered to be effective in a particular school yet being pushed towards a 'permeation' approach within an activity area-driven PE programme? It is also an interesting anomaly that the DFE considered 'dropping' PE from the 14 to 16 age range school curriculum (KS4) at a time when the DoH was becoming involved in the promotion of physical activity – physical activity was being promoted in one government department yet being cut back in another. Perhaps this explains the apparent U-turn between the Dearing interim and final reports based on the need for 'fit and healthy young people' (Dearing, 1993). However, having narrowly escaped the 'chop' at KS4, the PE profession needs to take a long hard look at KS4 PE in terms of its educational value, relevance and appeal, and the quality of the preparation it provides for the transition from organized school PE to the adult free marketplace.

Third, in 1994 it was announced that the Sports Council was no longer to be involved with the development of mass participation in physical activity and health promotion. Instead, it was to concentrate its resources on helping grass-roots sport, public health aims being considered to be secondary to the pursuit of high standards of sporting achievement (Department of National Heritage [DNH], 1994). Further, the formation of the Youth Sport Trust in 1995 has tended to similarly focus attention on the promotion of sport for young people, sport tending to be narrowly defined

It is not yet clear as to who is to take on the 'abandoned' role of mass participation and health promotion, although there have been significant positive moves from within health-associated organizations such as the HEA and the Health Service. However, the PE profession needs to consider whether it could play a more significant public health role with respect to promoting mass participation in health-related physical activity.

WHAT IS MEANT BY A HEALTH FOCUS IN PE?

A consensus definition of health-related fitness (HRF) is that it is fitness characterized by a person's ability to perform daily activities with vigour and to demonstrate traits and capacities that are associated with low risk of hypokinetic diseases and conditions (Bouchard and Shophard, 1991), examples of the latter being coronary heart disease (CHD), osteoporosis, obesity and back pain. Within the educational context in England and Wales, the term health-related exercise (HRE) has been adopted, this being defined as the knowledge, understanding, skills and attitudes associated with positive health and well-being through short- and long-term participation in physical activity.

HRE is imparted through enjoyable exercise experiences, a practical knowledge base, and caring teaching strategies. The exercise experiences should be varied, involving lifetime and individual activities as well as more conventional ones. The knowledge base should include the psychological and social effects of exercise on the individual and on society, as well as the physiological effects of exercise on the body systems (and not just the cardiovascular system). The teaching strategies should focus on the individual and develop the necessary behavioural skills associated with exercise adherence.

There is also a need to take heed of research findings that consistently report that girls are less active than boys (Cale and Almond, 1992) and that girls find competitive experiences less appealing than boys (Goudas and Biddle, 1993). It is also important that the PE profession is aware of its own contribution to pupils' confusion about appropriate exercise practices amidst the range of mixed messages they receive inside and out of school about health-related behaviour (Harris, 1994b). In particular, young people seem ill-informed about the potential role of physical activity in the maintenance of a healthy body weight. This is more than unfortunate given the health concerns associated with the steady increase in the percentages of adults and children who are overweight and obese in England (Sports Council and HEA, 1992).

Although HRE is now written into the NC, interpretation of the HRE statements remains very broad. In effect, HRE means different things to different people. To some, HRE is a central focus of the PE programme while for others it remains an afterthought tagged onto the activity areas. HRE may conjure up images of fitness testing, cross-country running, aerobics, circuits and skipping, in which children may be involved in vigorous activity and are encouraged or forced to 'huff and puff' or 'heave and pull'. Others may see HRE as predominantly associated with safety and hygiene issues such as warming up and cooling down, lifting and carrying equipment, and having showers after lessons. Some teachers identify a knowledge base associated with HRE and aim to impart learning through activity. Others, however, deliver activity-based units (eg, 'blocks' of aerobics, cross-country and circuit-training) without imparting any HRE learning concepts.

The general picture from a recent survey of 1,000 secondary schools in England is that most schools are delivering some form of HRE (sometimes called 'health-related fitness' or simply 'fitness') but that which is delivered varies tremendously between schools (Harris, 1994a; 1995). Grass-roots support for a specific health focus in PE seems to be strong, with more than half of PE heads of department stating that they would have preferred that HRE were placed within its own activity area, especially at KS4. Furthermore, only a minority of PE heads of department considered that HRE could be delivered through the activity areas alone at KS3 (less than a third) and at KS4 (less than a fifth). The reality was that as many as two-thirds of secondary schools were teaching HRE in focused units either at KS3 or KS4 or both, often in combination with teaching HRE through the PE activity areas. While over 80 per cent of secondary schools were teaching at least some HRE through the PE activity areas, less than 10 per cent used this as the sole method for delivering HRE. However, only a third of PE heads of departments described the overall teaching of HRE as structured, particularly that delivered through the PE activity areas.

Where a theoretical base for HRE was acknowledged, it focused predominantly on basic concepts associated with stamina, strength and flexibility. However, it was not clear whether this theoretical base represented a rationale for the inclusion of particular activities within the curriculum, or whether the theoretical concepts associated with stamina, strength and flexibility were being delivered to pupils during the lessons. It was far less common for HRE programmes of study to include any information about designing personal exercise programmes or about the role of physical activity in maintaining a healthy weight. The health education recommendations for HRE were generally unknown or overlooked and liaison with a health education coordinator (where one existed) was often limited. The survey suggests that many teachers were unaware or unsure about the HRE 'knowledge base', resulting in it being underestimated and that, where knowledge was imparted, it tended to be primarily physiologically based, such as focusing on pulse counting. Psychological and social issues were almost totally absent despite the wealth of information available about young people's perceptions of exercise (Harris, 1994b), their reasons for being active or inactive, and the behavioural skills associated with adopting and maintaining exercise behaviour (Sallis, 1994).

HEALTH-RELATED ISSUES

A major issue relates to the approach adopted to the teaching of HRE. How can HRE best be delivered? Should HRE be permeated through the activity areas or should it be taught in focused units of work? Certainly the absence of an activity area for HRE has been interpreted by some physical educators as indicating that HRE should be delivered in a particular way, through the PE activity areas, not in discrete 'blocks' or units of work (Oxley, 1994). Indeed, personal contacts with teachers over the past few years has revealed that some teachers have been 'strongly urged' by their PE advisers to abandon their HRE units of work and to deliver it in a 'permeated fashion' through the PE activity areas. Yet it is said that the NC is about content, not delivery, and that it allows scope for professional judgement regarding how best to transmit content within the context of particular schools. Indeed, the view that there is only one way to deliver HRE and the related assumption that this approach is effective has been strongly challenged (Harris and Almond, 1994). Furthermore, it is evident that not all PE advisers, inspectors and lecturers consider that HRE should be delivered within a 'permeation' model: the BAALPE has consistently reported that the current provision for HRE needs to be addressed, and that there should be a more definite emphasis on discrete HRE, particularly at KS3 and KS4 (BAALPE, 1994).

A prudent response to questions about how the teaching of HRE should be approached might be that the most effective response is the one that works best in any particular school. The critical issue is the effectiveness of the learning rather than the particular approach adopted. It is possible for a well structured and coordinated approach involving permeation through the activity areas to work. Equally, it is possible for a series of focused units over a Key Stage to be an effective way in which to deliver HRE. Indeed, it is known that there are a range of possible teaching approaches, the most common approach (adopted by a third of secondary schools in England) being one in which HRE is delivered in focused units of work in PE, as well as through some or all of the PE activity areas, and in other areas of the school curriculum (Harris, 1994a; 1995). This combined approach seemingly has the advantage of focusing on HRE concepts through a range of activities (conventional and otherwise), maintaining valuable links with the PE activity areas and other subjects, and minimizing the possibility of HRE being taught in isolation to other practical experiences in PE.

Concerns have been expressed about the low level of moderate to vigorous physical activity in PE lessons (Curtner-Smith *et al.*, 1995). While it is accepted that many PE lessons could be made more active for pupils (eg, by reducing time spent listening and queueing) and that this is desirable in terms of cardiovascular health benefits and pupil involvement and enjoyment, the issue of increasing activity levels in PE lessons raises several potential concerns. First, HRE appears to be viewed as merely involving children in vigorous 'huff and puff' activity, which certainly is the opinion of at least one Office for Standards in Education (OFSTED) inspector (Oxley, 1994). HRE is a multi-faceted concept involving the development of health-related knowledge and understanding, physical and behavioural skills, and positive attitudes towards physical activity.

Second, there are health benefits to be gained from involvement in moderate intensity exercise. Indeed, the forthcoming national promotion focuses on the benefits of moderate activity (ie, activity that leaves the individual warm and slightly out of breath) as does the proposed 'health standard' within the recent children's exercise prescription (Corbin *et al.*, 1994). While vigorous activity may provide more health benefits than moderate activity, an important message in terms of public health is that vigorous activity is not necessary for cardiovascular health benefits nor for weight management. Indeed, moderate activity is associated with improved adherence and reduced risk of injury.

Third, there are health benefits to be gained from activity types other than cardiovascular activity, such as exercises to enhance flexibility, muscular strength and endurance, and relaxation. Although CHD reduction is the primary aim of much physical activity promotion, it is unwise to overlook other important health benefits such as reduced risk of osteoporosis, back pain and depression.

Finally, there is a concern that some PE teachers may respond to reports of low activity levels of children by forcing children into 'hard' exercise, such as more cross-country running or fitness testing. Rather than aiming for short-term fitness gains, it is preferable that teachers increase the level of activity, involvement and interest of their pupils during PE lessons while at the same time developing their competence, confidence and desire to be active now and in the future. A 'hard-line' approach is likely to be counter-productive in the long term.

The study by Curtner-Smith *et al.* (1995) further reported that teachers allocated no time for pupils to engage in fitness activities or receive fitness knowledge, and teachers spent no time directly promoting or demonstrating fitness. This is consistent with my own research findings that the teaching of HRE through the activity areas was predominantly unstructured (Harris, 1994a; 1995). However, there may be an issue associated with the application of the observational instrument within PE programmes in England. For example, it is not clear what exactly comprises 'fitness activities' or 'fitness knowledge' and what is entailed in the 'promotion or demonstration of fitness'. Despite sound intra-observer reliability checks within the study, it would seem that some of the coding categories are not necessarily mutually exclusive. For example, where pupils were physically active, the activity had to be coded as 'fitness activity' or 'skill practice/game play'. It seems possible for pupils to be engaged in active skill practice that also enhances fitness and may, in a game-related warm-up situation, also contribute to fitness knowledge (eg, asking pupils to be involved in a low intensity activity with the ball followed by a few appropriate stretches). It may be that in other countries, 'fitness education' is more clearly delineated from 'skill education' than it is in England and Wales. Although I do not advocate this separation between 'fitness' and 'skill', the Curtner-Smith *et al.* study (1995) clearly highlights the potential limitations of a 'permeation' model for the delivery of HRE. Indeed, Curtner-Smith *et al.* suggest that secondary school physical education in England remains largely unaffected by the HRF movement and it is proposed that, in terms of their health-related contribution, different activities are assessed and new methods for teaching such activities are designed.

Perhaps the issue of seemingly contradictory messages regarding HRE will be clarified in the future as, in a recent review of school inspection findings, it was acknowledged that HRE may take place either as a separate area of work or be embedded within and permeating the aspects of the programmes of study, and that there is a need to recognize and record good practice in HRE wherever it occurs (OFSTED, 1995).

A second major health-related issue relates to fitness testing. Should schools include fitness testing within the PE curriculum? This is an important question given that fitness testing in schools has been criticized on the basis that (a) fitness tests are considered to merely expose the obvious in terms of varying levels of physical maturity within the same chronological age-set; (b) school-based fitness tests are relatively crude measures of the components of fitness; and (c) children' s fitness is not a major issue as children have been found to be as fit today as in the past (Armstrong, 1989). The anomaly of apparently stable fitness scores alongside allegedly decreasing activity levels is explained by the fact that fitness scores are influenced as much by inherited characteristics (such as an efficient cardiovascular system) as by the benefits of physical activity over a relatively short lifespan.

Recent surveys reveal that about 60 per cent of schools include fitness testing within the PE curriculum, and that much of this is compulsory for the lower age groups (Harris, 1994a; 1995). Little is known, however, about its purpose, style of delivery or effect. In order for fitness testing to maintain its place within the school curriculum, it needs to be justified on sound educational principles. However, it would seem that few teachers are aware of the professional guidelines relating to fitness testing (Physical Education Association, 1988), which strongly advocate that fitness testing be health-related, individualized, positive and educational in the sense that health-related learning concepts are delivered during the fitness testing process. A good example of such an approach to fitness and activity monitoring is presented in the Exercise Challenge (McGeorge, 1993), which is described in the next section. Fitness testing scenarios that remain a concern are those that are far removed from sound educational practice, examples being fitness testing without any associated learning and minimal or no follow-up guidance; public testing situations involving exhausting maximal tests often with no prior practice; and public comparison of test scores of pupils at different stages of growth and maturation, the latter undoubtedly reflecting their varied test performances.

In the USA, where physical fitness testing of school children is the most commonly used form of assessment in PE (Hopple and Graham,

1995), Rowland (1995) is of the opinion that such testing is archaic, inconsistent with current understanding of the exercise-health connection, and antithetical to the goal of promoting physical activity. He argues that fitness tests are demeaning, embarassing and uncomfortable for at-risk sedentary children and represent a negative experience that will turn youngsters 'off' rather than 'on' to physical activity. These views are supported by Hopple and Graham's study, which found that most pupils generally showed little or no understanding of why they perform fitness tests and many pupils viewed tests as painful negative experiences to be'dodged' where possible.

A further concern relating to fitness testing in PE lessons is the amount of time that may be spent on it without necessarily positively influoncing pupils' activity levels or their attitudes towards involvement in physical activity. Given the tendency towards reduced PE time in schools (Harris, 1994c), it is important that PE time is used wisely and, if the objective of fitness testing is primarily to increase activity levels, it would seem more logical to increase pupils' awareness of their own activity levels, of the recommended levels for their age, and of opportunities to be active at school and in the local community. It may be that extracurricular physical activity opportunities in school and outside of school need to be increased for pupils who could be described as relatively inactive, unfit, overweight, less able, uncoordinated or clumsy. More for the more able is unlikely to contribute significantly to public health.

HEALTH-RELATED INITIATIVES

A number of health-related initiatives have been developed over the past five years that focus on increasing understanding of health benefits and on helping more young people to be more active more often. The 'Active School', the 'Exercise Challenge' and 'Vitality' are examples of effective school-based health-related initiatives.

THE ACTIVE SCHOOL

The Active School is a national promotion to encourage schools to formulate and implement an action plan for increasing the participation of pupils in physical activity, both within and outside of school (Almond and McGeorge, 1995). Children's low activity levels and a decline in PE time over the past few decades have meant that PE has shifted towards more emphasis on stimulation of further participation in physical activity beyond PE lesson times.

The overall aim of an Active School policy is to increase the proportion of young people participating in physical activity, both inside and outside of school. Related objectives include forming action plans to increase physical activity amongst pupils, staff and parents, and the initiation of healthy alliances that facilitate the promotion of HRE in young people. Key principles underpinning the Active School philosophy are that all individuals should be valued and respected and that there should be sensitivity towards and tolerance of individual differences, needs and interests. An Active School should promote:

Activity	...that is...
Fun	...that leads to...
Achievement	...that brings...
Recognition	...and promotes...
Self-worth.	

There are numerous initiatives that schools could adopt in order to increase physical activity levels; some of these include:

- increasing the activity levels of PE lessons (eg, by reducing team sizes)
- ensuring differentiation in PE lessons so that all children can succeed
- ensuring that competitive experiences are positive and fair
- individualizing exercise experiences
- designing a sports day that involves every pupil (eg, through personal challenges, group activities and games)
- monitoring fitness and activity levels in and out of school (eg, using diaries)
- organizing participation challenges such as the '1,000 Club'
- organizing festivals on specific activities (eg, dance, games, skipping)
- introducing 'taster' sessions for pupils to try out new activities
- introducing participation award schemes (eg, gaining points for activity)

114

- encouraging a wide variety of playground activities (eg, with a 'card box' of ideas and/or an equipment box; through playground markings)
- organizing open-access weekend activities (eg, 'Saturday Morning' sessions)
- organizing special activity promotions (eg, Jump Rope for Heart 'Jump Off').

THE EXERCISE CHALLENGE

The Exercise Challenge is a scheme that encourages young people to be more active, helps deliver the HRE requirements of the NC, provides an opportunity to reward pupils for positive health behaviour, and helps promote links between teacher, pupil and parent. The scheme is detailed in a teacher's manual and is accompanied by pupil booklets (McGeorge, 1993). Initially, pupils are involved in completing an exercise profile in which they consider their current activity levels and take part in simple fitness monitoring procedures such as recovery pulse rate after exercise, modified curl ups and push ups, and a 'sit and reach' flexibility measurement. The fitness monitoring procedures are designed to be non-threatening, informative and individualized, and the emphasis is placed on current activity levels rather than fitness scores.

After the initial profile, 9–13-year-old pupils embark on a four-week Exercise Challenge, which involves them following a prescribed exercise programme. For the 14–18-year-old age group, pupils are assisted in designing their own six-week exercise programme. Each prescribed exercise programme contains a balance of cardiovascular activity (stamina), muscular strength and endurance exercises (strength), and flexibility exercises (suppleness). The level of the programme in terms of frequency (how often), intensity (how hard) and duration (how long) is determined by the baseline activity level of the individual pupil. For example, a pupil who currently exercises less than once a week would follow an easier exercise programme than a pupil who currently exercises three times a week or more.

The exercise programmes are designed so that the frequency and duration of the exercise gradually progress over the weeks. Pupils are provided with a wide choice of cardiovascular activities (eg, brisk walking, skipping, swimming, cycling, dancing) and examples of different levels of exercises to develop muscular strength and endurance, and flexibility. The intention is that pupils participate in some of the activities during PE lessons and are encouraged to complete the rest of the programme in their own time.

Pupils record their exercise in a diary that is signed by an adult (teacher, parent, guardian) at the end of each week. After the required number of weeks, pupils compare their own activity levels with those prior to starting the Exercise Challenge and they repeat the fitness monitoring procedures. Pupils are engaged in a simple evaluation of personal differences between recordings and are encouraged to consider the benefits of an active lifestyle. All pupils who complete the four- or six-week Exercise Challenge are rewarded with a certificate. The Exercise Challenge certificate is intended to reward positive exercise behaviour (ie, remaining with the exercise programme) rather than changes in fitness monitoring results.

The major benefits of the Exercise Challenge as an award scheme are that:

- it is attainable by all pupils
- it links with the NC
- it rewards effort and behaviour, not performance and natural talent.

VITALITY

Vitality is a project that focuses on helping individuals to enjoy physical activity, to enjoy eating well and to feel good about themselves. The aim of the project is to 'combat the tyranny of thinness' that tends to encourage people to value females primarily on their looks and that, in turn, puts pressure on females to respond by 'pleasing the eye'. Females tend to be sensitive to the opinions of others and thus are vulnerable to media messages about personal appearance. The solution sought is often for the individual females to attempt to lose weight, the consequence of this being large numbers of discontented young people who are dieting unnecessarily, for cosmetic purposes only. However, the solution is not that simple. There is a need to focus on tackling the media regarding such issues, and on helping young people to deal with media messages and to feel good about themselves while being active and eating well.

Based on research with young people, primarily females, a resource pack has been developed that is centred around messages relating to activity, eating and self-perception, and describes effective teaching approaches for delivering these messages. Currently the resource pack is being piloted with different sample groups: young people, teenage girls, and young female ethnic populations. Other potential target groups may include the adult population and the elderly.

CONCLUSION

The past seven years have witnessed major developments in children's exercise and health including acceptance at government level that physical activity is a desirable health behaviour and should be promoted from a young age. However, the Sports Council and the PE profession both seem to have been reluctantly drawn towards a greater focus on 'team games', which is a concern where it may impinge upon opportunities to increase mass participation in health-promoting physical activity.

The 'ascendancy of HRE' within the curriculum has been duly recognized (Green, 1994), the major foci of HRE being concisely summarized as helping children to understand how to 'keep actively healthy' and to develop in them a desire to do so. However, the wide-ranging interpretations of the HRE requirements within the NCPE and the inconsistent guidance from within the PE profession have led to a situation in which HRE represents anything from letting children do their own warm up now and again to putting in a block of aerobics or weight training for older pupils. There is undoubtedly much to be done in terms of clarifying the purpose, content and effectiveness of HRE in schools.

It may be that the apparent resistance to or ambivalence about HRE from within the PE profession stems from images of what might be described as poor quality HRE courses that are either predominantly activity-oriented (eg, blocks of totally directed aerobics, cross-country or circuit training) or are dominated by fitness testing. To the best of my knowledge, neither of these approaches have been advocated or encouraged by those delivering HRE inservice training. Indeed, it has been a major objective to shift teachers away from teaching approaches that involve any or all of the following: an over-emphasis on testing; 'directed "huff and puff" activity with minimal learning'; 'lots of teacher talk'; or, 'a whistle-stop tour of the "three Ss" (stamina, strength and

117

suppleness)'. The potential effectiveness of HRE should not be limited by judgements based on such courses but on quality HRE courses that represent a practical common-sense approach to preparing young people for 'active living', that is, a way of life in which physical activity is valued and integrated into daily life (Fitness Canada, 1991).

Statements made by the DoH (1992; 1995) and the Sports Council and HEA (1992) suggest that much faith is being placed in school PE to educate children about exercise and to activate young people. This requires genuine commitment and good quality HRE courses backed up by appropriate resources and training. The teaching of HRE appears to be shifting from the superficial and piecemeal approaches of the past towards more structured, meaningful and effective approaches. However, there is still some way to go on the road towards school PE significantly contributing to public health.

NOTE

Additional information about the Active School, the Exercise Challenge and Vitality can be obtained from: The Exercise and Health Research and Development Group, Loughborough University, Loughborough, Leicestershire, LE11 3TU.

REFERENCES

Almond, L and McGeorge, S (1995) *Leicester Health – An Active Schools Promotion,* Loughborough University, Leicestershire: Exercise and Health Group.

Armstrong, N (1989) 'Children are fit but not active!', *Education and Health,* 7(2), pp.28–32.

Armstrong, N and Bray, S (1991) 'Physical activity patterns defined by continuous heart rate monitoring', *Archives of Disease in Childhood,* **66**, pp.245–7.

Armstrong, N, Balding, J, Gentle, P and Kirby, B (1990) 'Patterns of physical activity among 11 to 16 year old British children', *British Medical Journal,* **301**, pp.203–5.

Bouchard, C and Shephard, R (1991) *Physical Activity, Fitness and Health: a Model and Key Concepts,* Consensus Doc-017, August 22; document prepared for the International Consensus Symposium on Physical Activity, Fitness and Health.

British Association of Advisers and Lecturers in Physical Education (BAALPE)

(1994), *BAALPE Newsletter*, Spring, pp.16–18.

Cale, L and Almond, L (1992) 'Children's activity: a review of studies conducted on British children', *Physical Education Review,* **15**(2), pp.111–18.

Corbin, C B, Pangrazi, R P and Welk, G J (1994) 'Toward an understanding of appropriate physical activity levels for youth', *Physical Activity and Fitness Research Digest Series,* **1**(8), pp.1–8. President's Council on Physical Fitness and Sports.

Curtner-Smith, M D, Chen, W and Kerr, I G (1995) 'Health-related fitness in secondary school physical education: a descriptive-analytic study', *Educational Studies,* **21**(1), pp.55–66.

Dearing, Sir Ron (1993) *The National Curriculum and its Assessment: Final report,* London: School Curriculum and Assessment Authority.

DFE and the WO (1995) *Physical education in the National Curriculum,* London: HMSO.

DES and the WO (1992) *Physical Education in the National Curriculum,* London: HMSO.

DoH (1992) *The Health of the Nation: A Strategy for Health in England,* London: HMSO.

DoH (1995) *The Health of the Nation. More people more active more often. Physical activity in England. A consultation paper,* Physical activity task force, London: DoH.

DNH (1994) *Sport for the 21st Century,* Paper DNH 101/94; dated 8 July, London: DNH.

Dishman, R K and Dunn, A L (1988) 'Exercise adherence in children and youth: implications for adulthood' in *Exercise Adherence: its Impact on Public Health,* R K Dishman (ed), Champaign, IL: Human Kinetics, pp.155–200.

Fitness Canada (1991) *Active living: A conceptual overview,* Ottowa: Government of Canada.

Goudas, M and Biddle, S (1993) 'Pupil perceptions of enjoyment in physical education', *Physical Education Review,* **16**(2), pp.145–50.

Green, K (1994) 'Meeting the challenge: health-related exercise and the encouragement of lifelong participation', *The Bulletin of Physical Education,* **30**(3), pp.27–34.

Harris, J (1994a) 'Health related exercise in the National Curriculum: results of a pilot study in secondary schools', *British Journal of Physical Education Research Supplement,* **14**, pp.6–11.

Harris, J (1994b) 'Young people's perceptions of health, fitness and exercise: implications for the teaching of health related exercise', *Physical Education Review,* **17**(2), pp.143–51.

Harris, J (1994c) 'Physical education in the National Curriculum: is there enough time to be effective?', *British Journal of Physical Education,* **25**(4), pp.34–8.

Harris, J (1995) 'Physical education: A picture of health?', *British Journal of Physical Education,* **26**(4), pp.25–32.

Harris, J and Almond, L (1994), 'Letter in response to OFSTED inspector's view of HRE in the National Curriculum', *The Bulletin of Physical Education,* **30**(3), pp.65–8.

Hopple, C and Graham, G (1995) 'What children think, feel and know about physical fitness testing', *Journal of Teaching in Physical Education,* **14**(4), pp.408–17.

McGeorge, S (1993) *The Exercise Challenge Teacher's Manual,* Loughborough University, Leicestershire: Exercise and Health Research and Development Group.

NCC (1990) *Curriculum guidance 5. Health education,* York: NCC.

OFSTED (1995) *Physical Education: a Review of Inspection Findings 1993/94,* A report from the Office of Her Majesty's Chief Inspector of Schools, London: HMSO.

Oxley, J (1994) 'HRE and the National Curriculum – an OFSTED inspector's view', *The Bulletin of Physical Education,* **30**(2), p.39.

Physical Education Association (PEA) (1988), 'Health-related fitness testing and monitoring in schools: a position statement on behalf of the Physical Education Association by its fitness and health advisory committee', *British Journal of Physical Education,* **19**(4/5), pp.194–5.

Riddoch, C J and Boreham, C A G (1995) 'The health-related physical activity of children', *Sports Medicine,* **19**(2), pp.86–102.

Rowland, T W (1995) 'The horse is dead; let's dismount', *Pediatric Exercise Science,* **7**(2), pp.117–20.

RCP (1991) *Medical Aspects of Exercise: Benefits and Risks,* London: RCP.

Sallis, J F (1994) 'Influences on physical activity of children, adolescents, and adults or determinants of active living', *Physical Activity and Fitness Research Digest,* **1**(7), pp.1–8.

Sallis, J F and Patrick, K (1994) 'Physical activity guidelines for adolescents: consensus statement', *British Journal of Physical Education Research Supplement,* **15**, pp.2–7.

Sleap, M and Warburton, P (1992) 'Physical activity levels of 5–11 year old children in England as determined by continuous observation', *Research Quarterly for Exercise and Sport,* **63**(3), pp.238–45.

Sports Council (1995) *Young People and Sport: National Survey Selected Findings,* London: Sports Council.

Sports Council and HEA (1992) *Allied Dunbar National Fitness Survey: Main Findings,* London: Sports Council and HEA.

CHAPTER EIGHT

The Active School

Sonia McGeorge

INTRODUCTION

The Active School is an initiative developed by Loughborough University in conjunction with the British Heart Foundation (BHF). It encourages teachers to formulate and implement an action plan for increasing the participation of their students in physical activity, both within and outside of school. The impetus for the development of the Active School was the recognition that despite evidence that physical activity can provide numerous health benefits, activity levels among young people appear to be declining.

It is acknowledged that schools have a very important role to play in promoting physical activity to young people and the Active School initiative was introduced to provide ideas and guidance for schools to increase participation among their pupils and to reward those schools that are providing an environment and opportunities conducive to high levels of participation in physical activity. Although much of the information included within this chapter relates to the BHF initiative, the principles and ideas are relevant to all schools that wish to make a commitment to promoting physical activity to all pupils, whether or not they intend to participate in this scheme.

Before outlining the aims and format of the Active School, the research underpinning its development and the context in which it has been developed are discussed.

RESEARCH EVIDENCE UNDERPINNING THE DEVELOPMENT OF THE ACTIVE SCHOOL

INFLUENCE OF PHYSICAL ACTIVITY IN CHILDHOOD AND ADOLESCENCE ON HEALTH AND WELL BEING

The positive health benefits of physical activity among adults have been extensively studied and are now universally acknowledged (Bouchard *et al.*, 1994; McGinnis, 1992; Powell *et al.*, 1989). The health benefits for the young are not yet clearly understood but there is still strong justification for promoting activity to this age group. The potential benefits of an active childhood and adolescence are two-fold, having a possible positive impact on both short-term and future health.

Short-term health
The short-term benefits of physical activity for young people are not completely understood but it is thought that physical activity may contribute to the following.

- *An improved coronary risk profile* with evidence that active and sedentary children differ in aspects such as adiposity (Bullen *et al.*, 1964), blood pressure (Fraser *et al.*, 1983; Strazullo *et al.*, 1988), glucose tolerance (Voors *et al.*, 1982) and plasma lipoprotein profile (Bell *et al.*, 1989; Gaul *et al.*, 1989).
- *The reduction and prevention of obesity,* which is important since obese children are more likely to have cardiovascular risk factors (Gortmaker *et al.*, 1987), are often less accepted by their peers (Buckmaster and Brownell, 1988) and often have a poor body image (Brownell and Stunkard, 1980).
- *An improved quality of life* with an active lifestyle contributing to an enhanced functional capacity that enables participation in a wider range of leisure pursuits and activity also shown to promote well-being, improve self-concept and self-esteem (Sonstroem and Morgan, 1989) and to be associated with lower levels

of anxiety and perceived stress (Dyer and Crouch, 1987; Norris *et al.*, 1991).

Future health
There is some controversy regarding the potential effects of regular participation in physical activity during childhood and adolescence on future health due to a lack of long-term studies, however, it has been suggested that long-term benefits may include the following.

- *Possible reduction of the risk of developing CHD* (Freedman *et al.*, 1985), a disease that was responsible for 150,000 deaths in 1994 (BHF, 1996).
- *Helping to prevent obesity* (Brownell and Kaye, 1982), which contributes to the development of many chronic diseases including CHD, stroke, selected cancers and Type II diabetes and is associated with osteoarthritis, gallstones, bronchitis and an increased risk associated with surgery.
- *Reduction of the risk of osteoporosis* (Slemenda *et al.*, 1991), a condition that results in about 6,000 hip fractures a year in the UK (HEA, 1995).
- *Increased possibility of an active adulthood* (Dennison *et al.*, 1988; Sports Council and HEA, 1992), which is important as the benefits of activity cannot be 'stored up' and the health benefits of activity and consequences of inactivity are well established for adults.

YOUNG PEOPLE'S ACTIVITY LEVELS

Evidence suggests that young people in Britain are relatively inactive, with activity levels having declined over recent years due to factors such as an increase in sedentary leisure time pursuits and fear for the safety of young people outside of the home.

Currently there is no large-scale survey on young people's activity levels comparable to the Allied Dunbar National Fitness Survey (Sports Council and HEA, 1992) carried out on adults; however, there are numerous small scale studies that provide useful indications of the activity habits of this age group. Some caution is needed in interpreting the available data as the methods used and definitions of 'appropriate' activity have been diverse.

123

Children
Studies have indicated that children of primary school age in Britain are not regularly participating in continuous activity of a moderate to vigorous intensity that is thought to be necessary to promote cardiopulmonary fitness (Armstrong and Bray, 1991; Sleap and Warburton, 1994). There is evidence that young children 'accumulate' significant amounts of activity each day through participation in repeated short bouts of activity of less than 10 minutes' duration (Sleap and Warburton, 1994). The benefits of accumulating such short bouts of activity are yet to be established in children, although recent recommendations from America for this age group do acknowledge the value of accumulating more moderate activity.

Adolescents
The most recent activity guidelines for adolescents (aged 11–20 years) recognize the valuable contribution of accumulated physical activity but also highlight a need for this age group to participate in sustained activity to accrue all the potential health benefits (Sallis and Patrick, 1994). Studies in Britain have revealed that many young people of secondary school age are not reaching these recently recommended levels of activity, in particular demonstrating few sustained bouts of continuous aerobic activity (Armstrong, 1989; Dickenson, 1987).

Future research may indicate that more frequent, shorter bouts of moderate physical activity may provide similar health benefits as the existing recommendations for adolescents. However, even if less stringent criteria recommending shorter bouts of moderate activity were appropriate, studies indicate that many adolescents would still be considered to be participating in insufficient levels of activity (Armstrong, 1989; Dickenson, 1987; Hendry, 1978).

OTHER BENEFITS OF INCREASED LEVELS OF PHYSICAL ACTIVITY

A fundamental reason for developing the Active School was the recognition that there is a need to promote increased participation in physical activity among this age group to maintain and improve the short- and long-term health of this and future generations. While the promotion of improved health and well-being is the central rationale for initiating the Active School, there are many other potential, equally valuable, benefits related to an increased participation in physical activity that are also likely to materialize. These include increased opportunities for young people to:

- experience fun, enjoyment and excitement;
- experience a sense of satisfaction in performing to the best of their ability;
- acquire skills, knowledge and attitudes to promote a lifelong participation in physical activity;
- make friends;
- be challenged, either on an individual level or through competition against others;
- learn to work together in a team environment;
- acquire a valuable foundation for the development of talent in all activities and sports.

THE CONTEXT

In recent years physical activity and sport have had a high profile in the media and there has been recognition at a national level that there is a need to encourage more young people to participate in physical activity and sport. The impetus to increase participation levels has come from both the health and sporting spheres with concerns raised over the future health and sporting prowess of today's young people. The need to promote physical activity and sport among young people has been acknowledged at government level and this has led to the development of a number of initiatives that have important implications for those involved in promoting physical activity and sport to young people. All of these have had an impact on the development of the Active School and the most influential are outlined below.

THE PHYSICAL EDUCATION NATIONAL CURRICULUM

The introduction of the Physical Education National Curriculum (DES, 1992) has led to schools being required to provide all pupils with a designated range of activity experiences and has meant that physical education has become an entitlement for all children aged 5–16 years. In addition to the designated activity areas, health-related activities are a

125

statutory requirement at each Key Stage, requiring pupils to acquire the knowledge, understanding and skills needed to pursue an active life through practical experiences of appropriate activities.

While the National Curriculum provides guidance on the content of physical education lessons, there is no stipulation regarding time allocation. A study by the Secondary Heads Association (SHA) in 1994 revealed that 75 per cent of those aged 14+ had less than two hours physical education a week and the time allocation for secondary schools appears to be the lowest in Europe (Harris, 1994). The findings of the SHA study led to the recommendation that there is a need for 'a government statement emphasizing the importance of adequate time provision for physical education'. This recommendation has now been made in *Sport – Raising the Game* (see below).

The NCC (1992) points out that the limited amount of curriculum time makes it impossible for pupils to experience a full range of activities; thus extracurricular provision can make a very valuable contribution in extending the activity experiences offered to young people. Extracurricular activities can also provide young people with a useful 'bridge' between participation within school and involvement in activities offered in the local community.

The non-statutory guidance for physical education (NCC, 1992) suggests the creation of opportunities to allow pupils to take some responsibility for running school clubs, assisting with coaching, leading sessions, umpiring matches and organizing tournaments.

THE HEALTH OF THE NATION

Increased awareness of the health benefits of physical activity has led to its being placed on the health promotion agenda. The profile of physical activity in the health sphere has been raised by the introduction of *The Health of the Nation* (DoH, 1992) and the subsequent formation of a Physical Activity Task Force.

The Health of the Nation, a Government White Paper that sets out a strategy for promoting health in England, has heightened awareness of the benefits of physical activity. One key area focused on in *The Health of the Nation* is coronary heart disease and stroke. Physical activity has an important role to play in reducing the incidence of these diseases both directly and through influencing other risk factors. Physical activity can also have beneficial effects on two of the other key areas identified within *The Health of the Nation*: 'mental health' and 'accidents'.

THE PHYSICAL ACTIVITY TASK FORCE

It is recognized that physical activity is likely to play a valuable role in reaching the national and regional health targets identified through *The Health of the Nation* and this has led to the establishment of a Physical Activity Task Force. The role of the latter is to develop a comprehensive physical activity strategy for England, focusing on encouraging participation in physical activity among the adult population. Tho first phase of this strategy has already been implemented with a national activity campaign, 'Active for Life', which was launched in March 1996, and further specific campaigns are likely to follow.

SPORT – RAISING THE GAME

Sport – Raising the Game was launched by the DNH in 1995 with the aim of encouraging and promoting sport so that the pleasure experienced by both participants and spectators can be maximized. According to John Major, the document has four central aims:

- to put sport back at the heart of weekly life in every school;
- to bring every child in every school within reach of adequate sporting facilities by the year 2000 and to protect our nation's playing fields;
- to enable sporting opportunities to continue after school in college and university and through better links between school and club sport;
- to develop excellence among the most talented of our sports men and women.

Two particularly important recommendations for schools made within *Sport – Raising the Game* are that two hours a week should be devoted to physical education and the need to make provision within extracurricular time to extend sporting opportunities for children.

A first year report published on *Sport – Raising the Game* indicates that it has already been the catalyst for change. Hopefully, further changes will continue to develop to convert many of the ideas put forward in this document into positive action.

SPORTSMARK

The Sportsmark and Sportsmark gold awards have been developed to give recognition and rewards to schools providing a quality physical education. To qualify for these awards, schools need to satisfy seven different criteria relating to the hours of timetabled physical education each week; the amount of organized sport provided outside timetabled lessons; the amount of time devoted to games both inside and outside timetabled lessons; the competitive opportunities provided for pupils; the access for teachers and others involved in extracurricular sport to coaching qualifications and awards; the establishment of links between schools and local sports clubs; and the participation of pupils in sports governing bodies' award schemes.

THE ACTIVE SCHOOL

It is against this background that the idea of the Active School was developed. Increasing recognition of the need to promote physical activity among young people provided the stimulus and the various initiatives outlined above have helped to shape the development of the Active School.

It is intended that the Active School will endorse the promotion of all types of physical activity and that it is relevant for all organizations involved in the promotion of physical activity and sport to young people, whatever their motivation. Although organizations involved in the promotion of sport and those involved in promoting health may have different priorities, ultimately their central aim is the same and that is to encourage more young people to be more active. Sports-based activities will make a positive contribution towards young people's health. Health-related activities such as swimming, jogging and circuits will provide a valuable foundation for involvement in sporting activities.

If all the potential benefits of physical activity are to be accrued by all young people it is evident that there is a need to promote activity in its widest sense, from individual, non-competitive activities through to competitive team games. Due to the all-encompassing nature of the Active School, positive contributions in all areas of physical activity and sport are possible and the aims and objectives outlined in many other documents such as Raising the Game, Sportsmark and National Governing Body strategies are all likely to be addressed.

WHAT IS THE ACTIVE SCHOOL?

The Active School:
- is a national promotion to encourage teachers to formulate and implement a policy and development plan for increasing their students' participation in physical activity (these could form the basis of the documentation required for OFSTED inspections);
- includes a resource document containing a comprehensive selection of existing and new practical ideas and resource information to help increase pupils' participation;
- includes a two-level recognition scheme that has been developed to reward those schools that are making a commitment to being an Active School;
- encourages liaison with other agencies including, for example, alliances with health promotion and sports development officers;
- encourages teachers to monitor and demonstrate their successes.

The Active School is intended to provide all teachers with a valuable resource to promote physical activity within and beyond their school whether or not they wish to participate in the recognition scheme.

AIMS OF THE ACTIVE SCHOOL

The overall aim of the Active School initiative is to make physical activity a better experience for more young people more of the time, thereby increasing participation rates both inside and outside of school. Four key aims have been identified to help meet this central objective:

- encouraging more pupils to be more active;
- providing pupils with positive physical activity experiences;
- ensuring that curricular physical education is a quality learning experience for pupils;

- catering for the needs of every child.

The following are considered an integral part of these:

- encouraging schools to adopt an active schools policy and formulate action plans to promote increased physical activity among pupils, staff and parents;
- providing a focus (and purpose) that embraces all forms of physical activity;
- promoting positive attitudes towards participation in physical activity;
- increasing pupils' knowledge and understanding of the importance of physical activity;
- encouraging teachers to adopt a new role to stimulate increased participation in activity by young people;
- providing a support structure for promoting more physical activity by more young people more of the time;
- initiating healthy alliances that will facilitate the promotion of health-related exercise in young people;
- increasing young peoples' knowledge and understanding of the importance of physical activity;
- stimulating an interest in, and positive attitude towards, physical activity, sport and exercise by young people.

CENTRAL FEATURES CONSIDERED IMPORTANT IN AN ACTIVE SCHOOL

There are a number of features that are considered central to the Active School philosophy and that are relevant to the achievement of the four key aims. It is hoped that all schools will strive to adopt these aspects, although it is recognized that this is likely to take time and in some cases may be impractical due to external requirements and restrictions.

General
It is hoped that an Active School would have or be working towards:

- a comprehensive Active School/physical activity policy;
- an appointed PE coordinator;

- a policy of including appropriate warm ups and cool downs for all activity sessions and a commitment to safe and effective exercise procedures;
- a high profile for physical activity throughout the school with established cross-curricular links;
- a strategy for promoting physical activity during breaks and lunchtimes;
- a programme that provides pupils with the information and confidence they need to independently take advantage of physical activity opportunities within the community;
- periodic promotions to raise the profile of physical activity, eg physical activity day;
- the involvement of other staff and parents with appropriate qualifications in leading extracurricular clubs or providing support.

In addition to these general aspects, there are features within certain areas of provision that are considered important; these are outlined below.

Curriculum
The following should be evident:

- a nominated person responsible for curricular provision;
- effective fulfilment of the National Curriculum requirements, both general and specific;
- a curriculum that caters for the needs of all pupils and provides equal opportunities for all pupils to participate and achieve in different activities;
- a curriculum that provides opportunities for all pupils to experience a range of activities, with each activity covered in a sufficient depth to enable pupils to gain a level of appreciation and understanding;
- utilization of appropriate resource packs to enhance activity opportunities offered to pupils;
- pathways from the curriculum into extracurricular and community opportunities that help pupils to pursue activities outside of school hours.

Extracurricular

The following should be considered:

- having a nominated person responsible for extracurricular provision;
- providing an extracurricular programme that is a natural progression from the curriculum, with activities offered in the curriculum being developed further and additional opportunities not covered in the curriculum being provided;
- providing an extracurricular programme that is varied and includes both individual activities (eg, circuits, aerobics) and sports-oriented opportunities (eg, team games);
- providing a range of opportunities that cater for the needs and abilities of all pupils, both the able and the less talented;
- provision of competitive opportunities for all those who wish to be involved in such experiences;
- establishment of links between extracurricular clubs and local centres/clubs to help pupils make the transition to independent participation in activity;
- the involvement of activity leaders from the community either to help provide extracurricular opportunities (if appropriately qualified) and/or to meet with pupils and introduce them to opportunities available in their centre/club;
- encouraging as many pupils as possible to take advantage of extracurricular opportunities.

Links with the community and other schools

The following should be considered:

- having a person responsible for liaising with relevant individuals within the community and other schools;
- developing links with local leisure centres, community organizations, sports clubs and youth services to help establish pathways from school-based activities through to community-based opportunities;
- involving activity leaders from the community either to help provide activity opportunities (if appropriately qualified), to provide 'taster sessions', and/or to meet with pupils and introduce them to the opportunities available in their centre/club;
- making information on activity opportunities in the community

readily available to pupils;

- arranging visits to local leisure centres to help pupils become familiar with these venues and the opportunities they offer;
- organizing informal meetings between local schools to provide opportunities to share ideas and experiences;
- establishing links between secondary schools and their feeder primary schools to help smooth the transition from one school to the next.

Training and resources
The following should be considered:

- provision of regular opportunities for all staff teaching physical activities to take part in relevant inservice training to help update practice and develop their knowledge and expertise in a range of activities;
- provision of adequate resources for all pupils to be actively involved in lessons and clubs, eg enough small equipment to enable small-sided or where appropriate individual activity without pupils having to wait.

KEY PRINCIPLES CENTRAL TO TEACHING IN AN ACTIVE SCHOOL

In addition to the central features outlined above, there are a number of key principles that should ideally guide practice and permeate all activity provision within an Active School. Aspects to consider include:

- providing all children with equal *access* to appropriate curricular and extracurricular programmes;
- providing all pupils with *equal opportunities* to participate and achieve in different activities;
- ensuring that all curricular physical activities have *integrity* with a clearly identifiable educational content;
- ensuring that there is *breadth* and *balance* in the curricular and extracurricular programmes;
- providing pupils with a physical activity experience that is *coherent* and *relevant*;
- providing a *differentiated* provision of physical activity that matches tasks to pupils different abilities, needs and interests.

WHAT IS INCLUDED IN THE ACTIVE SCHOOL?

Section 1: The Active School Recognition Scheme
The Active School Recognition Scheme is designed to reward those schools who are making a commitment to promoting participation in physical activity among their pupils. There are two levels of the award: the 'Active School Award' and the 'Advanced Active School Award'. Ten core elements and 11 additional elements thought to be indicative of an Active School have been identified (comprising many of the central features outlined above). To qualify for either of these awards schools are required to complete an audit that outlines their current provision and demonstrates that they are fulfilling a set number of core elements and additional elements.

The Active School Recognition Scheme has been designed to complement and extend the Sportsmark Scheme and fulfilment of the Active School Award or Advanced Active School Award will help contribute to achievement of the Sportsmark and Sportsmark gold award. There is inevitably overlap between the two awards. Schools achieving the Sportsmark or Sportsmark gold awards will have also fulfilled some of the criteria for the Active School Recognition Scheme; however, to be eligible for an Active School Award, schools will need to satisfy broader requirements.

The focus in the Sportsmark and Sportsmark gold awards is on quality sports provision; such provision is considered an important aspect within the Active School Recognition Scheme. However, this is only one aspect and schools also need to demonstrate that they promote other physical activities such as dance, gymnastics, aerobics and circuits to qualify for an Active School Award.

Section 2: The menu of possibilities
This provides teachers with practical examples of ways in which they can encourage pupils to become more active. Both new and existing ideas are outlined. Although some new ideas are introduced, the intention is to help make teachers aware of the plethora of valuable ideas and resources available and encourage them to maximize the impact of these through developing a comprehensive action plan. The section is divided into three parts:

- initiatives that could be incorporated into curriculum time;
- possible developments for pupils in the extended curriculum

including:
- — activities to enhance the curriculum and link to extracurricular time
- — initiatives to promote activity at breaks/lunchtime
- — extracurricular activities
- — promotions
- — links with outside agencies and local sports clubs;
- • strategies to involve parents and other staff.

Examples of the ideas presented in each of these sections are outlined below.

Initiatives for the curriculum

The framework for the content of the physical education curriculum is defined by the statutory requirements of the National Curriculum; however, the method of delivery is not stipulated and this can have a significant influence on the effectiveness of physical education lessons in motivating pupils to increase participation.

The programme of activities offered within the curriculum should:

- • provide all pupils with positive physical activity experiences by ensuring that tasks set are appropriate for the age and ability of each particular group;
- • help pupils acquire the skills and knowledge they need to enable them to participate in a variety of activities;
- • help move pupils from dependence on the teacher to independent action.

The examples presented by Rod Thorpe, Len Almond and Lorraine Cale in this book illustrate ways in which games, athletics and gymnastics can be presented to maximize pupil participation and enjoyment.

Possible developments in the extended curriculum

Activity challenges provide one way in which links can be established between the curriculum and extended curriculum; these could be participation or skills based.

To encourage pupils to participate frequently in activity, a range of challenges focusing on participation could be set up. Targets could be set:

- • for individual pupils to achieve as a one-off event or as part of an ongoing process;

- to form the basis of an inter-form or inter-house challenge (with pupils and staff both taking part) – this could be a special event organized periodically to encourage more pupils to be active.

Targets could be based on:

- accumulated 'mileage' – from activities such as walking, running, cycling and swimming;
- accumulated number of minutes/hours spent participating in activity;
- accumulated number of skips for skipping (or jump roping);
- highest total 'mileage', number of minutes/hours or number of skips accumulated in a set period of time (for inter-form/house challenges).

In all cases it is important to stipulate the maximum amount of activity that can contribute towards a pupil's total on one day and over the duration of a week to ensure that pupils do not attempt to participate in excessive amounts of activity in a short time period. This will help to reduce the risk of injury and increase the probability that pupils will continue with the activity in the long term.

Examples of participation challenges include '100 mile club', 'Run around Britain' and '1000 Skips Challenge'.

Levels of activity during breaks and lunchtimes are often low, with only a minority of pupils participating in active games. There are a number of ways in which activity can be promoted at breaks and lunchtimes. The extent to which these are introduced is likely to be determined by the age of the pupils and availability of resources. Steps that can be taken include:

- organizing a 'Playground Games Card Box' with examples of games pupils can try;
- providing a games equipment box;
- providing appropriate playground markings;
- encouraging pupils to practise activities they have tried in lessons;
- designating certain areas/times for certain activities;
- introducing activity challenges;
- focusing on active playtimes on specific days.

Extracurricular activities tend to be dominated by sports teams and matches (Mason, 1995; Sports Council for Wales, 1993) with a limited number of pupils taking part. One possible way of encouraging increased levels of participation outside of school hours is by introducing participation-based clubs. Possibilities include:

- games based activities with an emphasis on participation and informal games;
- individual activities such as exercise to music and circuits;
- taster sessions of a range of more unusual activities (these could be offered in association with local clubs and/or leisure centres);
- clubs focused on working towards the achievement of a sport/ activity challenge (like those described on pages 135–6) or an award scheme.

Promotions at particular times of the year can help to raise the profile of physical activity generally or help to focus on a specific activity. One possible promotion is a physical activity day or week, which could include:

- organizing special activity clubs before school, during lunchtime, after school and in the evening;
- including unusual activities in physical education lessons;
- inviting outside instructors to lead some activity sessions;
- encouraging pupils to walk/cycle to and from school (safety aspects need to be carefully considered first);
- promoting cross-curricular links through encouraging the support of other staff;
- providing activity sessions for staff and parents after school;
- providing more 'healthy' food options at lunchtimes.

Strategies to involve parents and other staff
Support and encouragement from parents is essential if pupils are to participate in activity outside of school. Examples of the ways in which parents could be involved include:

- providing them with an information leaflet/booklet;
- inviting them to a physical activity/sports day;
- involving them in the provision of extracurricular activities.

The impact of an Active School will be greater if all those working at the school support and promote the initiative. Some examples of ways in which staff outside the physical education department can be involved include:

- developing cross-curricular links;
- providing activity sessions for staff;
- inviting staff to help with extracurricular activities.

Section 3: Useful information
This section is a valuable reference document providing information on existing award schemes, mini games, and training courses and relevant resources for teachers. A summary of the relevant options provided by many of the main activity and sporting organizations is provided.

SUMMARY

Sport and physical activity have increasingly been in the spotlight in Britain and there is a need to capitalize on this high profile to encourage young people to become more active. Many organizations are involved in promoting physical activity and sport to young people and government documents such as *The Health of the Nation* and *Sport – Raising the Game* should help to reinforce the valuable work these organizations are doing. The Active School acknowledges the value of all types of physical activity. While the promotion of health is the primary objective, the many other benefits provided by sport and physical activity are recognized and valued.

Schools play a vital role in encouraging more active lifestyles among young people, but they cannot achieve this alone. Liaison with outside agencies and parents is essential if the end goal of increased lifelong participation is to be achieved.

REFERENCES

Armstrong, N (1989) 'Children are fit but not active!', *Education and Health*, **7**(2), pp.28–32.

Armstrong, N and Bray, S (1991) 'Physical activity patterns defined by continuous heart rate monitoring', *Archives of Disease in Childhood*, **66**, pp.245–7.

Bell, R, Macek, M and Rutenfranz, J (1989) 'Blood lipoprotein profiles in trained and untrained adolescents' in *Children and Exercise XIII*, S Oseid and K H Carlsen (eds), Champaign, Ill.: Human Kinetics.

Bouchard C, Shephard, R J and Stephens, T (1994) *Physical Activity, Fitness and Health – International Proceedings and Consensus Statement*, Champaign, Ill.: Human Kinetics.

BHF (1996) *Statistics Factsheet*, London: BHF.

Brownell, K D and Kaye, F S (1982) 'A school-based behaviour modification, nutrition education, and physical activity program for obese children', *The American Journal of Clinical Nutrition*, **35**, pp. 277–83.

Brownell, K D and Stunkard, A J (1980) 'Physical activity in the development and control of obesity' in *Obesity*, A J Stunkard (ed.), Philadelphia: Saunders.

Buckmaster, L and Brownell, K D (1988) 'The social and psychological world of the obese child', in *Childhood Obesity: a Biobehavioural Perspective*, N A Krasnegor, G D Grave and N Kretchmer (eds), Caldwell, NJ: Telford Press.

Bullen, B A, Reed, R B and Mayer, J (1964) 'Physical activity of obese and non-obese adolescent girls appraised by motion picture sampling', *American Journal of Clinical Nutrition*, **14**, pp.211–23.

Dennison, B A, Straus, J H, Mellits, E D and Charney, E (1988) 'Childhood fitness tests: Predictor of adult physical activity levels?' *Pediatrics*, **82**(3), pp.324–30.

DES (1992) *Physical Education in The National Curriculum*, London: HMSO.

DoH (1992) *The Health of the Nation*, London: HMSO.

DNH (1995) *Sport – Raising the Game*, London: DNH.

Dickenson, B (1987) *Survey of the activity patterns of young people and their attitudes and perceptions of physical activity and physical education in a Local Education Authority*, MPhil thesis, Loughborough University.

Dyer, J B and Crouch, J G (1987) 'Effects of running on moods: a time series study', *Perceptual Motor Skills*, **64**, pp.783–9.

Fraser, G E, Phillips, R L and Harris, L R (1983) 'Physical fitness and blood pressure in schoolchildren', *Circulation*, **67**, pp.405–12.

Freedman, D S, Shear, C L, Shrinivasan, S R, Webber, L S and Berenson, G S (1985) 'Tracking of serum lipids and lipoproteins in children over an 8-year period: the Bogalusa Heart Study', *Preventive Medicine*, **14**, pp.203–16.

Gaul, C A, Docherty, D and Wenger, H A (1989) 'The effects of aerobic training on blood lipid profiles of young females', *Canadian Journal of Sport Science*, **14**, p.112.

Gortmaker, L, Dietz, W, Sobol, A and Wehler, C (1987) 'Increasing pediatric obesity in the United States', *American Journal of Diseases of Children*, **141**, pp.535–40.

Harris, J (1994) 'Physical education in the National Curriculum: is there enough time to be effective?', *The British Journal of Physical Education*, **25**(4), pp.34–8.

HEA (1995) *Health Update 5: Physical Activity*, London: HEA.

Hendry, L B (1978) *School sport and leisure – three dimensions of adolescence*,

London: Lepus Books.

McGinnis, J M (1992) 'The public health burden of a sedentary lifestyle', *Medicine and Science in Sports and Exercise*, **24** (supplement), pp.S196–S200.

Mason, V (1995) *Young People and Sport in England, 1994*, London: Sports Council and OPCS.

NCC (1992) *Physical Education Non-statutory Guidance*, York: NCC.

Norris, R, Carroll, D and Cochrane, R (1991) 'The effects of physical activity and exercise training on psychological stress and well-being in adolescent population', *Journal of Clinical Psychology*, **36**(1), pp.55–65.

Powell, K E, Caspersen, C J, Koplan, J P and Ford, E S (1989) 'Physical activity and chronic disease', *American Journal of Clinical Nutrition*, **49**, pp.999–1006.

Sallis, J F and Patrick, K (1994) 'Physical activity guidelines for adolescents: consensus statement', *Pediatric Exercise Science*, **6**(4), pp.302–14.

Secondary Heads Association (1994) *Enquiry into the Provision of Physical Education in Schools*, London: CCPR.

Sleap, M and Warburton, P (1994) 'Physical activity levels of preadolescent children in England', *British Journal of Physical Education Research Supplement*, 14, pp.2–6.

Slemenda, C W, Miller, J Z, Hui, S L, Reister, T K and Johnston, C C Jr (1991) 'Role of physical activity in the development of skeletal mass in children', *Journal of Bone Mineral Research*, 6, pp.1227–33.

Sonstroem, R J and Morgan, W P (1989) 'Exercise and self esteem: rationale and model', *Medicine and Science in Sports and Exercise*, **21**, pp.329–37.

Sports Council and HEA (1992) *Allied Dunbar National Fitness Survey main findings*, London: Sports Council.

Sports Council for Wales (1993) *Children's Sport Participation 1991/2*, Cardiff: Sports Council for Wales.

Strazullo, P, Cappuccio, F, Trevisan, M, De Leo, A, Krogh, V, Giorgione, N and Mancini, M (1988) 'Leisure time physical activity and blood pressure in school children', *American Journal of Epidemiology*, **127**, pp.726–33.

Voors, A W, Harsha, D W, Webber, L S, Radhakrishnamurthy, B, Srinivasan, S R and Berenson, G S (1982) 'Clustering of anthropometric parameters, glucose tolerance and serum lipids in children with low B- and pre-B-lipoproteins: Bogalusa Heart Study', *Atherosclerosis*, **2**, pp.346–55.

CHAPTER NINE

Revisiting the Key Stage 4 curriculum

Bernard Dickenson

INTRODUCTION

There has been enormous attention given to the physical education curriculum (NCPE) during the past few years in the development of the National Curriculum. Much of this has been directed at the curriculum for Key Stages 1–3, where issues associated with swimming, dance, health-related exercise and, more latterly, games have exercised the minds of all of those involved with the subject.

Two of the least debated features of the curriculum have been:

1. The model upon which the NCPE is based. This develops movement experiences in the early years into a broader basis of knowledge and performance in activity areas, brought together in later years into specialization at KS4.
2. Due to the revisions to the order for PE and the staggered dates for the implementation of the Key Stages, the curriculum for KS4 has probably received the least attention of any of the Key Stages. While on the one hand this is understandable, due perhaps to more immediate priorities, the KS4 curriculum, in both

141

its intentions and implementation, is a significant departure from that previously experienced by students.

The purpose of this chapter is to set out those factors impacting on the KS4 curriculum and to offer some practical solutions for consideration.

THE KEY STAGE 4 CURRICULUM

There has been an assumption that because we now have a National Curriculum, which provides content requirements, there is little else to be concerned about in relation to KS4. However, as in previous years there are a number of other factors, which continue to influence the curriculum. The following are a few examples.

THE VOCATIONAL CURRICULUM

The development of the vocational curriculum is making a significant impact on the way schools and colleges prepare students for the world of work. The expansion over the past few years of vocational courses (GNVQ and NVQ) in the post-16 sector has been remarkable. At the same time, it has become clear that the GCSE study route is inappropriate for many young people pre-16. The more recent development of Part 1 GNVQ courses for students in years 10 and 11 will provide a coherent, progressive route through to employment or advanced study. As these courses continue to develop and flourish there will be a uniform acceptance of their merit, quality and rigour, so that they will not be perceived as only for the less able. There is no doubt that the vocational curriculum will continue to grow over the next few years and will make, in particular, a consistently strong contribution to the KS4 curriculum. These courses, due to their structure and design, will also make a significant impact on teaching and learning styles and assessment strategies and procedures.

GCSE PHYSICAL EDUCATION

GCSE courses are currently being revised to satisfy National Curriculum requirements. GCSE physical education has been the fastest growing course for candidates over the past four years (Hodgson, 1996; OFSTED, 1996). It now appears to be more popular than subjects like, for example, music, information technology or physics. The greatest relative increase in course candidature between 1994 and 1995 was in physical education and science: single award (Fig. 9.1). There has also been a 20 per cent increase in the number of candidates in 1995 for physical education to 68,114. In 1994 there were 50,500 Year 11 candidates for physical education, in England, which represented 9 per cent of the student cohort (SCAA, 1995).

While there are some relatively minor differences between different examination boards syllabuses, there are a number of significant similarities. For example, all boards include theory and coursework. The theory is assessed using a written examination and the coursework is assessed 'practical performance'.

Most boards include some aspects of the following topics in their theory component: anatomy and physiology, exercise and fitness,

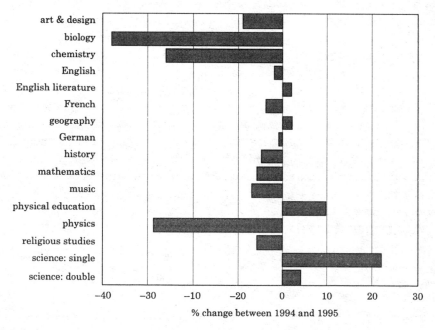

Figure 9.1 Proportional changes in GCSE candidature between 1994 and 1995.

143

training, safety and injury, and reasons and participation. Practical work is assessed by the school and subsequently moderated. Most boards require students to be assessed in at least four activities. Usually, these have to be taken from three of the National Curriculum activity areas.

Clearly, these courses provide a well rounded, relevant area of study, which fulfils the National Curriculum requirements for physical education. The potential difficulty they cause to schools is the requirement for students to be assessed in activities from three National Curriculum activity areas, ie games, gymnastics, dance, athletics, swimming and outdoor and adventurous activities. The problem is that, depending on the KS3 curriculum, some students may have little experience in some of these activity areas before starting the course. In addition, some of the activities may require significant resourcing in terms of either time, equipment or expertise. While these problems are not unsolvable, they do place restrictions on some schools to deliver the course, and could disadvantage some students in achieving high standards.

GCSE PHYSICAL EDUCATION (GAMES)

More recently, there has been the development of a GCSE Physical Education (Games) course. A number of boards have published syllabuses for first examination in 1998. As with the other physical education course, it includes theory and practical components. The theory is usually exactly the same as the other PE course. The practical component usually requires students to be assessed in at least four different games from the three games types, ie invasions, net/wall, striking/fielding. The advantages of this course are that it also satisfies National Curriculum requirements and it may prove to be more manageable for schools, in that there is less need to provide a broader basis of student expertise.

It will be interesting to see how successful this course proves to be. In time, because of the similarities, some schools may wish to run both courses and decide at a later stage which course a student is likely to be entered for, based on their practical strengths.

GCSE 'SHORT COURSES'

The development of 'short courses' at GCSE level may have a significant impact for subjects like PE, as it is becoming increasingly likely that all study at KS4 will lead to accreditation. Involvement in these courses may also secure an acceptable time allocation for the subject, as well as assist with National Curriculum compliance. However, at this stage the uptake of 'short courses' generally has been modest.

ACCREDITED COURSES

For a number of years there have been courses of work accredited by a validating body, which recognizes student achievement. The growth of these courses within the areas of sport, leisure and health has been nothing short of remarkable. The following are just some examples of sport governing body awards that have a minimum age of 16 and are therefore possible for most students to obtain by the end of KS4:

> Badminton Leaders Certificate
> Basketball Leaders Award
> Basketball Referee Award
> British Canoe Union
> Closed-Cockpit Kayaks
> National Cricket Association Coaching Award
> FA Football Leaders Course
> British Amateur Gymnastics Coaching Awards
> Class Awards
> Hockey Association Leadership Awards
> Keep Fit Association Coaching Awards
> Amateur Rowing Association Coaching Awards
> Squash Rackets Association Teachers and Leaders Awards
> Amateur Swimming Association Preliminary Teaching Awards
> English Table Tennis Association Sportsleader Awards
> English Volleyball Association Level 1 Coach
> Royal Yachting Association Dinghy Instructor

It is very likely that these courses will play a much more significant role in the KS5 curriculum and begin to play a part in the KS4 curriculum. These courses will enable students to improve their personal performance in specific activities, while also being able to address other aspects of National Curriculum end of Key Stage descriptors, for example: undertake different roles, such as performer, coach, choreographer and official; evaluate accurately and make judgements using relevant technical terms. In addition, the course of study, if accredited, can be added to the student's personal portfolio of achievements.

SCHOOL INSPECTIONS

Another factor that cannot be ignored is the development of a national programme of school inspection. Probably the major impact of this has been to focus attention on standards of student achievement and the quality of teaching and learning. There are significant implications for the KS4 curriculum in PE as traditionally students have been introduced to unfamiliar activities with an approach that is characterized by recreative participation. The combination of these two traditional features of the curriculum does not necessarily encourage good standards of achievement and attainment. It should be noted that the National Curriculum programmes of study require students to demonstrate competence in, for example, 'increasingly advanced strategies and tactics of competitive play... increasingly advanced techniques in a selected game and how to improve performance'. It is unlikely that a student will be able to demonstrate this level of competence if they have only been introduced to an activity during KS4. Therefore, to fulfil National Curriculum requirements and the expectations of inspectors, the PE programmes for students will have to be carefully structured to provide an appropriate balance of depth and variety.

Furthermore, OFSTED has indicated in its inspection findings for 1995/6 a number of important issues for school physical education departments to consider. It is perhaps predictable that the development of effective systems for assessment and the delivery of health-related activity should appear as issues. However, there are other issues that relate to KS3, but will impact on KS4. For example, schools are cautioned about introducing too many new games activities in years 8 and 9, and teaching them in short blocks of time, as this may hinder the development of high standards. Significantly, OFSTED also comments on the practice of mixed gender games teaching in KS3. They suggest that schools should reconsider carefully its effectiveness.

These are important issues when there is an emphasis on pupils achieving high standards. Some schools and their PE departments might have to reconsider their aims, intentions and strategies for teaching and learning in the light of this 'new' focus.

THE KEY STAGE 4 PHYSICAL EDUCATION – PRINCIPLES

Before looking at the practicalities of implementing the KS4 PE curriculum, it is important to consider certain principles that underpin this Key Stage. The first concerns the aims of the curriculum. Most PE departments will have aims that can broadly be categorized as the development of a range of physical skills, fostering personal and social qualities and promoting active lifestyles. Of these, probably the one most frequently associated with KS4 is promoting active lifestyles.

A significant number of studies indicate that the physical activity patterns of young people are a cause for concern (Cale and Almond, 1992). If we are to genuinely promote this aim, the KS4 curriculum must be relevant to the needs, aptitudes, interests and abilities of the students and must be taught in a way that will encourage self-esteem and independence, based on a sound performance and knowledge base.

The role of the physical education curriculum needs to be clearly articulated; the intention must be motivating young people to be physically active in their own time, not just providing activity during school time. It is vital that real links are made with the 'community' so that a genuine partnership is established with local sports/recreation clubs, youth organizations or community projects. Initiatives like Champion Coaching can play an important role in providing participation links between the curriculum and sporting independence. It is also important to recognize that promoting these aims need not be within the domain of discrete PE time. A more holistic view of the curriculum should be promoted so that more efficient use of time and expertise is made.

CONCLUSION

In presenting the issues and challenges to be faced in planning the KS4 physical education curriculum, three strands emerge:

Strand	Characteristic	Potential outcomes
Practical	development of personal competence	independent participation
Academic	development of a wider knowledge/performance base	GCSE accreditation
Vocational	development of community role and career route	GNVQ, CCPR, etc. accreditation

All three of these strands should be recognizable in the KS4 curriculum. However, differences will exist in the weighting given to each strand, based on the practical and philosophical decisions made during the planning process. It is hoped that these decisions will be better informed by a clear view of the issues and potential for the curriculum that this chapter has attempted to set out. The KS4 curriculum in physical education should lead students towards a personal portfolio of achievement in sport, leisure and health-related areas. This portfolio should reflect the interests and aptitudes of the student and provide evidence of achievement and attainment that has personal value as well as a potentially wider currency or credibility for vocational or academic study.

However, the main issue for PE departments to consider has been identified in the recent survey of good practice, conducted by OFSTED (1995), in which it identified the need for schools to consider what measures they could take to create a more structured course of study at KS4 for all pupils. This statement clearly indicates that the recreative programme of activities is a thing of the past and that schools must begin to embrace the National Curriculum model for physical education in both spirit and content.

REFERENCES

Cale, L and Almond L (1992) 'Children's activity levels: a review of studies conducted on British children', *Physical Education Review,* Autumn, **15**(2), 111–18.

DFE (1995) *Physical Education in the National Curriculum*, London: DFE.

Hodgson, B (1996) 'Which exam?', *British Journal of Physical Education*, Summer, **27**(2).

OFSTED (1995) *Physical Education and Sport in Schools – A Survey of Good Practice*, London: OFSTED.

OFSTED (1996) *Subjects and Standards. Issues for school development arising from OFSTED inspection findings 1994–5. Key Stages 3 and 4 and post-16*, London: OFSTED.

SCAA (1995) *GCSE Examinations Results*, London: SCAA.

Kogan Page books provide practical examinations of current issues in educational management and policy. Make sure you keep abreast of changes – see below for just some of our new and forthcoming titles. More information is available from the Marketing Department at the address below.

Development Planning and School Improvement for Middle Managers
Marilyn Leask and Ian Terrell
£16.99 Paperback ISBN: 0 7494 2038 3

500 Tips for School Improvement
Sally Brown and Helen Horne
£15.99 ISBN: 07494 2230 0

Pathways to Adult and Working Life: Curriculum Planning for Teaching and Learning
LENTA (London Enterprise Agency)
£99.00 Ringbinder ISBN: 0 7494 2380 3

Dearing and Beyond: 14–19 Qualifications, Frameworks and Systems
Edited by Ann Hodgson and Ken Spours
£14.99 Paperback ISBN 07494 2160 6

A Whole-School Behaviour Policy
Roy Lund
£18.99 Paperback ISBN: 07494 2058 8

Strategic Planning for School Managers
Jim Knight
£16.99 Paperback ISBN: 0 7494 1726 9

Kogan Page Ltd
120 Pentonville Road
London N1 9JN
Tel: 0171 278 0433
Fax: 0171 837 6348
e-mail: kpinfo@kogan-page.co.uk